25p

Sera 2012

Someday I'll Find Me

Someday I'll Find Me
CARLA LANE

Her Frank & Captivating Autobiography

**ROBSON
BOOKS**

First published in Great Britain in 2006 by
Robson Books
151 Freston Road
London
W10 6TH

An imprint of Anova Books Company Ltd

ISBN 1 86105 973 6

10 9 8 7 6 5 4 3 2 1

Typeset by SX Composing DTP, Rayleigh, Essex
Printed and bound by MPG Books Ltd, Bodmin, Cornwall

This book can be ordered direct from the publisher
Contact the marketing department, but try your bookshop first

www.anovabooks.com

To my wonderful family, my sons Carl and Nigel, my Sister Marna, Leonard, my Brother Ramon and my beautiful Grandchildren.
To Doreen, a dear friend.
To Chrisy my tolerant typist.
To Candi, our office guru, always there for Animaline.
To Anne, who runs our Animal Shop.
To Ian, Yvonne and Mark, my comrades in the fight against live animal exports.
To Lyndsey de Paul for goading me to write this book.
To all those who work at Broadhurst Manor and in the Sanctuary.
To all other animal people.
And to 'Norman', the big black spider in my bath!

CONTENTS

Chapter 1

BEGINNINGS

I came into the world with important advantages: my mother, Ivy Amelia Foran, who was eighteen, and my father, DeVinci Barrack, who was nineteen and in the Merchant Navy. They loved each other noticeably until he died when he was fifty-one years old. So I was brought up in a happy family world with my brother Ramon and my sister Marna. I was not a beautiful child – my two front teeth were crossed and my hair was totally disobedient – but in my bedroom I was anything I wanted to be.

My father brought many things home from sea; among them were a tambourine and a silk Chinese gown. I used to drape the gown over my head, pretending that it was long and that I had curl-laden hair and smouldering eyes. I would tap the tambourine with the back of my hand the way Jean Kent did in the film *Madonna Of The Seven Moons*, and I saw in the mirror what I wanted to be.

My father was a romantic man, so I was able to confide in him the fact that soon I would be running off to Spain to be a dancing gypsy. He smiled and ruffled my hair. 'That's fine,' he said, 'as long as you don't mind emptying the cockroaches out of your shoes each morning.' So ended my dream.

I never joined in the laughter and child-like screeching which so often came from our garden. My brother and our friends playing leapfrog, and pushing each other into the paddling pool was not right for me. Instead, I sat on the back-door step rescuing the earwigs which kept falling into the dog's drinking dish. Every time I fished one out with a leaf a little shudder ran through me, I didn't like the way they sneakily raised their pincers over their backs nor the strange malformed shape of their body, but I just could not turn myself away from their struggle. Looking back, I now know so clearly that this is the way I began my life and that it will be how I end it.

I began my school life in a Liverpool convent. My father, who was not a religious man was still at sea and my Catholic mother took advantage of the fact that the convent was just across the road.

Each morning, after prayers, the child who had said their prayers with eyes closed tight and hands clasped, were chosen to wear a little silver medal with the Virgin Mary engraved on it. My greatest childhood wish was to wear that medal, my eyes and fingers hurt as I kept to the rules and, each morning, somebody else was chosen.

One day, during playtime, when everybody was occupied outside, I crept along the endless stone corridor, with its carved angels and plaques bearing the names of those deceased, flowers and burning candles. I came to the largest statue of Our Lady. She stood on a huge marble shelf, with her hands together in prayer and her head slightly bent forwards so that you felt that she was truly listening to you. I was just about to tell her about my need to wear the medal when a hand clutched my wrist. It was Sister Maria. 'What are you doing?' she asked harshly.

'I . . . I . . . I . . .'

'You are not of our religion,' she said. 'You have no right to be talking to Our Lady.'

She dragged me along the corridor towards the nuns' staff room and then she said, 'I am going to cut off your hands.'

When we arrived at Sister Teresa's office, I was sobbing and struggling. 'She's going to cut off my hands,' I shouted.

Sister Teresa sat motionless for a moment, and then in her quiet, gentle voice said,

'Will you please go, Sister, I will attend to this.'

I remember her gentleness, but I forget exactly what she said. Soon afterwards, she took me back to the classroom and there were a few whispered words between her and the teacher, Sister Josephine. Then she left. After all this, the teacher and the rest of the class were particularly nice to me.

A few days later, we were saying our morning prayers when my father, just a few hours home from sea, came busting into the classroom. I recall the astonishment on Sister Josephine's face as he took my hand and dragged me towards the door. He didn't speak a word, but on the way out he swept everything off Sister Josephine's desk – the inkwell, the Bible, everything. Outside, he hugged me. 'You'll never go back there, sweetheart,' he said.

Next, I went to the village school. It was a small building made of great Welsh stones. It was about a mile away, and each morning, together with lots of others, I would walk straight along the road that led to the village and the school. I can see it now: little groups of children with satchels, bright scarves and bobble hats, laughing and pushing each other and, at the gates of the school, Freddie, the cocky Watchman as we called him – small, frail and very, very brown. He had hardly any teeth and wild black hair. He would greet each one of us at the gate of the school, touching each shoulder and saying 'That's you in, that's you in.'

After we arrived, Assembly took place in the schoolyard; each class stood separately with its own teacher – ours was Miss Trumpet. We eventually stopped laughing at her name as we grew accustomed to it. She was exceedingly fat and wore a brightly coloured silk coat over her other clothes. Even her hair was wild and bush like. She was a harsh but fair-minded lady. She noticed right away how the boys giggled at my chest during PT, and she would command the whole boys' class to move to the other side of the yard.

School was full of fear for me. I was aware of my scholarly shortcomings and my inability to take the whole business of learning seriously, but the thread of something, which turned out to be words, was manifesting itself. Each year, the entire school held a special day when the pupils were asked to contribute something which they had made or designed. It was always mostly knitting, dressmaking or embroidery. I, of course, ignored the whole thing until the day the Lady Mayoress arrived to judge our efforts. The whole of Class Room 4 had been turned into a display place for all the contributions. There were some beautiful things there – knitted garments with fine, satin bows, embroidered tray cloths and cushion covers, linen tablecloths with lace edges and sometimes flowers and animals embroidered on them. I was panic stricken – I went into the cloakroom and wrote a one-verse poem. I do not remember the words properly, but I know it was about the red leaves which gathered round the outside toilets. This I knew much about because, while the teacher was giving a lecture, I would turn my face to the window and watch these autumn leaves springing, gathering in little piles here and there and then dispersing again. I attached this grubby piece of paper to one of the boards next to a rather lovely little knitted matinee coat. Suddenly, I heard my name – I received a five-shilling prize – I could not believe it – and neither could anybody else.

When I was just nine years old, a most frightening thing happened. Grandma's bungalow was on the banks of the River Dee, which was a tidal river. One summer's day when my father was home, he, my mother and my grandma decided to take a walk across the sand dunes while the tide was out, and I pleaded to go with them. We walked for over a mile, until we came to the deep, cool pools that the tide used to leave behind when it went out, and Daddy and I spent ages pushing each other in and playing around. While they were setting up a picnic, I walked over a mound of wet sand and I noticed there was water all around us. I ran back and told my father, not thinking that it was at all serious. Immediately, the picnic was abandoned. My grandma began to cry, saying 'Oh Vinci, Vinci, we're trapped.' My mother was silent. Daddy ushered us all over the mound and he knelt down in front of me. He said, 'I want you to be a brave girl – I want you to stay here while I take Mummy and Grandma across. I'll be very quick and you mustn't be frightened because I will come back for you.'

I wasn't really very bothered – I didn't understand the grave danger we were in. I don't know how my father did it. I watched him for quite some time. My mother and grandma seemed to be hanging on to one of his arms as he swam with the other, at least that's how it seemed. As I stood there, the water came up to my feet. It felt quite warm and safe, and I thought, 'I'll get across myself.' I started to walk into it – I was already feeling proud of the idea of crossing by myself, –but suddenly a great swirl of water played around my legs. The current was rushing towards the sea – I couldn't stand up and I couldn't get back. I was beneath the water – it was like being in a washing machine – and I was being churned round and round and up and down. Now and then I glimpsed the sky – I must have taken a breath but I don't really recall. There were bubbles everywhere and at some point my feet seemed to be in front of my face. I don't remember being terrified – I just felt as if it were all a dream. There was a strange whirring noise as the water rushed around me, and I seemed unable to think anymore. The next thing I knew, I was lying on the sand; my mother was crying and my grandma was wringing her hands and saying 'Oh Vinci, Vinci,' and Daddy was holding me close, saying 'You'll be all right sweetheart, you'll be all right.' What had happened was that a fisherman, who was looking for cockles, saw me enter the water and he came out and rescued me. My father met him some of the way and I was told that the poor fisherman wouldn't come out of the water because he'd taken all his clothes off to save me. Since then, I have always been terrified of water, and in spite of the fact that I took that journey in a fast moving gulley, I have never been able to bring myself to swim or even to paddle.

Apart from that nightmare, I enjoyed my young years. With my father away so much, my mother suffered badly from loneliness, so we went to and fro from one set of grandparents to another while he was away.

On my mother's side the surname was 'Foran.' Granddad Foran was also a seafarer and served as a chef on the *Britannic*. He was Irish and he was never sober. My grandma, however, adored him.

Times with them were exciting. There were no rules about bedtime, or making too much noise, or roller-skating up the hall to the kitchen, where Granddad kept his sacred apple pies. He guarded these like a soldier and made a great ceremony of giving us each a small piece.

The front door of their house opened directly onto the street and it was never shut. I loved the street. It was a place of skipping ropes, balls being banged against walls, roller-skates, marbles and lots of beloved grandmothers and grandfathers sitting outside each front door in battered armchairs. They wore shawls and brand new slippers and were showered with love and affection. The women all wore wide, gold bands on their wedding fingers and the men all looked like the men in van Gogh's paintings.

Grandma Foran was mobile and bright. She always looked so young. One day, I asked her why. She replied, 'Your face is as young as the thoughts in your head.' Grandma Foran would never sit outside their front door – she said it was a common thing to do.

At night, with the streetlights turning our little bedroom yellow and my brother asleep on his knees, his head buried in the pillow, I used to listen to the people coming home from the pub, singing a rather darker version of 'Oh She Was a Milkmaid'. This invariably meant old Tom joining in, who said that he was the son of a famous tenor. He never said which one, but whichever one you suggested to him, he agreed that that was he. His rendering of 'O Sole Mio' was heartbreaking. I think it was the Liverpool accent and the well-presented tears that gave it its poignancy.

There were fights, too – I used to get out of bed for those. It was often the Mock family – they were bonded together with what seemed like an anchor chain, but now and then, there was a struggle to be top thug, and the street was filled with the sound of family wrath. Best of all, was Mrs Higgins. She would drag her daughter by the hair out into the street and with a terrifying Scottish accent, she would cry, 'Away with yer, you tart, you are no daughter of mine.' Then anticipating rebellion, she would very quickly and with excellent slight of hand, remove her dentures and slip them into her apron pocket. This would go on all night, and mother would come up to the room and make me close the window. 'Back to your bed,' she would order, 'what would your father, out at sea, say if he knew if you were filling your head with grown-up nonsense.' And still outside the air would be ringing with mothers calling 'Harry, get in here, it's late,' 'Where's our Mary, she never washed her face today,' 'Where's our

Stanley, he trod on my clean step this morning, and Mary never combed her hair – oh she's turning into a proper hussy.' And then it was nearly dawn and silence – the streams of black smoke rising from the chimneys would lose themselves in the dark grey night and the moon would slip behind those same chimney pots, lending us long moments of shimmering light. How I loved the noise of it all, the passion of it all, the sheer ugliness of it all.

Memories of Liverpool and family live in my mind wherever I am and whatever I'm doing. Having been brought up in Liverpool, a place of complexity, a place where people seem to have a gene of their own, perhaps these thoughts come from the memory of my father and my grandfather – of going up the gangplank to greet them with their wooden chests full of wonderful things from all over the world – silken gowns, embroidered fans and fragile, painted tea sets. My grandfather, in particular, would bring home animals. Our wash house, as it was always called, and which was simply an outside building within the yard, was filled with strange creatures: snakes, lizards and birds of every kind and every wonderful colour. He used to bring them home for friends who eagerly awaited his return, standing ready with their homemade hutches, sheds and cages. Once, he actually brought home a donkey – I remember he coaxed it into the wash house, there to stay until one of his friends collected it. Another time, for his own amusement, he brought home a little monkey sitting on his shoulder, and as fast as he hung up these great bunches of bananas on the clothes rack, the monkey threw them down one at a time at anybody who entered the room. These lovely moments soon ended as regulations, rules and laws came into being – and rightly so I feel. When Granddad could no longer bring these things home, Grandma's passion came into being and our wash house was full of singing canaries which were bought in Liverpool.

Granddad Foran died when I was nine. His non-stop drinking finally took its toll and he died of liver cancer. Grandmother Foran died in her bed several years later. I was the one who found her. My mother had asked me to take her up a cup of tea. She was wearing her little pink bed jacket and a couple of dinky curlers in her soft hair. She had been reading a book and – I don't know why I remember these two things – but it was open on page fifty-six and the book was called *The Last Pinnacle*.

The Barrack side of the family was different. Granddad Barrack was an artist and a recognised poet. In his younger days, he was the Chief Inspector of the RSPCA and had a great love for animals. He also had a rather quick temper. Grandma Barrack was a softly spoken lady – she was pretty, I remember, and once I peeped into a little tortoiseshell box on her dressing table and inside were strands of pale brown hair attached to a clip. These, I realised, were what she wore during the daytime. She also wore strangely eccentric clothes made of silk, velvet and soft materials that billowed around her. Mealtimes were polite rituals, using the silver cutlery that had my granddad's initials engraved on each item. He also wore eccentric clothes – a velvet smoking hat, a silk waistcoat and a little embroidered jacket. His favourite time was early in the morning, going to the end of his garden. There was a flower-laden balcony overlooking the sea. He used to raise his binoculars and watch the terns land on the sand before the tide came in, and he waited quietly for them all to rise suddenly and leave. I confess with sorrow and shame that often I would run to the orchard, which also overlooked the sea, and clap my hands before he reached the terrace, causing the birds to rise and him not to see them. 'Damn you! Damn you child,' he would shout and I would run away, shamefully I admit, laughing.

My grandfather and I had many little conversations in his study – I always remember how awesome he looked, and I was never sure whether or not he was going to be angry with me. One day, we were standing before the picture entitled 'The Coming of the Storm'.

'Why are all their clothes blowing, Granddad?' I asked.

'Wind, child, weather.'

'Why don't they have shoes on?'

'They are in the clouds, can't you see? You don't need shoes up there.'

'I don't like it, I wouldn't have it in my house.'

He would bang his walking stick on the floor. 'I'm quite sure it wouldn't like *being* in your house. Now, off you go, and pull your knickers up, child.'

Granddad Barrack died when I was twelve years old. He was sitting in his great oak chair with his hands clasped and his beloved binoculars on his lap. He looked asleep, the way I had often seen him. I felt no sadness then, but since have felt much. My biggest regret was that I was too young to understand him, or to please him. It is now that I wish I could have another conversation with him. But he left me with a great love of animals and art. I do have a large picture of 'The Coming of the Storm' in my own house. And something he didn't know, but which would please him, is that when the fishermen used to put the boxes of live fish on the beach, I used to creep down and pick up the struggling fish and take as many as I could back to the sea.

There is one other person I must mention – Auntie Gertie. She was Grandma Barrack's sister and throughout our childhood days spent at the bungalow, she was always there – quiet – secret – sitting on the big, carved wooden seat in the orchard. She wore a long grey plait down her back and she always wore brown, dark brown. Sometimes for days she would go without speaking a word – the only time she really spoke was when a little bird landed near her and she would say 'Off you go, little bird, go quickly now before someone harms you – off you go.'

It seems that she married a soldier when she was twenty-three years old and he was killed three weeks later. Her grief was overwhelming and she was trapped by it. She went into a local church, the one in which they were married, and stole the gold chalice from the altar. This brought great shame on Grandmother Barrack, who was proud and 'posh'. Somehow, she couldn't forgive her sister for it, but as Auntie Gertie had nowhere to go, she gave her a tiny bedroom at the back of the bungalow. I wish now that I had asked about Auntie Gertie. Instead, we regarded her as just strange, if not funny, and I am ashamed to say that we often laughed at her. Many years later, of course, after she died, I look back on this lonely lady's life and am made angry by the thought that I never spoke to her. She died in that little room in the bungalow. I was told that she was sitting in her one chair beside the bed and on her knee was a little wooden box with a painting of a robin on the lid, inside which were just a few coppers, all she owned.

Being thirteen years old was not a particularly enjoyable time for me. The onset of puberty embarrassed me. No one else had breasts in my class and the boys kept nudging each other, especially when I was skipping. I failed miserably in the school exams, and I was now spending much of my time secretly writing tortured poetry. My mother sent one of these poems to the *Liverpool Echo* and they published it. A great flurry of excitement broke out among the family. My mother could not have done any better with a loud hailer. She toured the district molesting people, the postman, the breadman, the milkman, the man who came to repair the road drains and anybody else who came within range of our home, waving the torn piece of *Echo* in front of them. She sang my praises like an old bell rings and in order to make sure her daughter's genius was clear, she persuaded my grandma to read it out in the Hall of Hope on Sunday.

It was while I was playing in the street that I met Johnny Graham. It was love, right away love. We were both the same age and my mother immediately went into why she didn't like him. Each time she heard his severely disabled bicycle coming up the path, she would remind me that he was a nice boy, but after all he was only a paperboy and paperboys, she said, were without ambition. She also mentioned that she had noticed that he wore string to hold his trousers up and that his boots were designed for goblins.

One beautiful, bright, wet afternoon, Johnny Graham kissed me. Little drops of rain fell on my face, I felt like Heddy Lemar. Seconds later, I watched him wobble off on his bike – he was Dante, I was Beatrice. The joys of love were snatched from me when two days later I saw him with Shirley O'Brien, my best friend, on his cross bar. 'There will be others,' said my mother, which I found quite touching, until she added, 'and maybe they won't be so common.'

By the time I was fifteen, I had abandoned school completely, apart from writing secret poetry. I regularly came thirty-fifth out of thirty-eight in every exam and my annual reports were doom laden. 'Romana Barrack is a poor scholar – she suffers from lack of concentration. She does however get on well with the class and has a keen sense of humour.' (In case you are getting confused, I should perhaps mention here that it was only when I started working for television that I adopted the name Carla Lane!) When a lady down the road offered me a job in her tiny baby-linen shop for a pound a week my mother couldn't refuse.

The shop was small and very close to home. It served all the local mothers. I was completely disinterested from the start – the idea of damp and screaming babies had not yet endeared itself to me. I spent my whole day helping mothers to choose a bonnet for their offspring. Bonnets in those days were over-embellished, the child's face became entombed in satin – there were bows everywhere and little ribbon rosettes. They were all purest white and did nothing to add to the wrinkled little face of a newborn and they were often not the right size because most mothers preferred them to be on the larger side. This meant that when the baby turned his head his face swivelled and disappeared, and one was left with an ear wearing a bonnet! Some babies actually suit a bonnet – those who are over a month old and have lost that over-cooked look. Anyone younger than that should avoid the bonnet and go in for a veil.

Apart from decorating their babies, the mothers were obsessed with knitting. They knitted all kinds of weird things for their offspring: baggy leggings, matinee coats, bootees, mittens, shawls – often I would gaze into a pram and there would be no sign of a baby as he was swamped in knitted things. I was soon bored with this work and swore that I would never engulf my babies in knitted objects – the truth being of course, that I couldn't knit.

My next encounter with the cruel world was through my employment in the Bon Marché, a terribly posh shop in the City of Liverpool. By this time, I had developed cheekbones and my face had arranged itself in a reasonably acceptable way, so I was put on the cosmetic counter. I suppose it was here that I learned much about the sadness of life; posh ladies, their youth gone, buying and wearing crimson lipsticks, thick pancake makeup, seriously black mascara and, for the sleeping hours, pink pots of lanolin-laden night cream. I remember one lady in particular, her face so laden with makeup that she looked rather like a tomato pizza. 'You my dear are at the start of life; don't do what I did and take the wrong turning,' she laughed and the sound was rather like the crows I heard in the park. Her smoker's chest sounded like a miniature volcano. She walked away, her tired legs throwing her from side to side, collided with the swing door, fought her way out, and disappeared. I have never forgotten her, although sometimes I have forgotten her advice.

One evening, on my way home, I leapt off the bus a stop too soon and found myself part of the moving mass of workers leaving their factories in Prescott Street. It was a new world, rough, with much cursing and shrill laughter, another kind of life. 'Aye Jack, did yer clock in for me?' . . . 'Aye I did.' 'If me Mam finds out I took the day out, she'll bloody kill me.' Laughter. Someone was behind me: 'Cummon, Queen, get your arse out of the way, I've got another bus to catch.' I moved to one side, she clanked past me in her huge shoes. 'See yer tomorra love – tarra.' A few steps, 'Oh God, me stockings are falling down.' She stopped, wriggled, hoisted and moved on. That was it – I wanted to work in a factory.

I was working on the assembly line putting telephone dials together. The strange thing was that my uncle had designed the dialling system. He was acclaimed in his day and received honours for his work, but these girls I now worked with would not be impressed with such trivia.

The girl on my right nudged me. 'My name's Josie,' she said. 'What did you say your name was?'

'Romana' I said with some embarrassment.

She gathered everybody's attention with her raucous voice 'Oh did yer hear that – Romana!' and then, turning to me, 'What was yer mother, a bleeding gypsy?' Laughter trickled along the assembly line and I joined in. Josie nudged me again, she pointed to a man, 'Yer see 'im, he's the chief.' This was a round, red-faced man with a stomach large enough to demolish all before it. 'Now,' said Josie, ''is name is Mr Hardcock and if anything goes wrong, love, you just put your hand up and call 'is name, OK?'

'OK,' I said.

It was only minutes later that the black-ringed dial, which had arrived on the conveyor belt for me to assemble, refused to fit, and I panicked: 'It doesn't fit.'

Josie calmly nodded towards the man she called the Chief. I put my hand up and shouted, 'Mr Hardcock.'

He thundered towards me, 'Yes, love?'

'This ring doesn't fit.'

He drew in a deep breath and almost whispered in my ear, 'Doesn't it now?' He looked along the line of straight-faced, busily working girls and said aloud, 'I wonder why?' He looked at Josie, 'I've told you, haven't I? If this happens again, you get the push, all right?'

I was very stressed at this point; I felt that somehow I had let somebody down. I desperately needed to succeed in this strange and basic world. Mr Hardcock was talking in my ear again: 'And by the way,' he said, 'my name is Woodcock not Hardcock, OK?'

I had been watching Eric Arthur Hollins as he skated round the ice rink. He was tall and graceful, his pale leather jacket suggested good taste. I stepped on to the ice in my navy-blue velvet ice-skating dress and new white boots. The intention was to hover round him gracefully and distract him from the blonde female hunter who was showing her feminine charm by breaking into frenzied pirouettes. I thought I would begin by attempting a nippy little leap, landing gracefully beside him and gliding away leaving him totally stunned.

He was waiting for me outside the first aid room. We left the rink with me limping badly, and the rain pouring down. He sheltered me beneath his jacket and our ice skates clanked together as we walked towards the bus stop.

Eric bought me a very impressive engagement ring. My parents were impressed and saw the ring as a gesture of longevity. I am still not sure whether or not the feeling I felt for Eric was love, as we know it, or the need to escape from all other ties and set out on a life of my own.

We were married six months later; I was seventeen, he was twenty. Our parents hated each other; his called mine 'toffee nosed,' mine called his 'common'. In order to stop a family mutiny, we decided to marry secretly.

St Jude's Church, known as the Church Of Hopeless Causes, was a dark-stoned building poised on a piece of raised ground which overlooked a very busy street leading to the city centre. The vicar's voice was lost in the huge, carved ceiling, and our 'I do's' were drowned out by the road drills outside. My bridesmaid was a new work mate whom I had only asked the day before, who said, 'Yeah, but I can't stay long because I've got to go to the chip shop 'cos I always get me granny's lunch on a Friday.' Eric and I walked together down the narrow aisle and stood in the entrance holding hands. The men who were working outside threw funny little kisses and made suggestive love gestures – and these were our only guests. But a passing motorbike, which seemed to have something wrong with its engine, drowned out even their antics. Its driver gave us a two-fingered sign and off we went in Eric Arthur's crippled car to London.

When we returned, we found a tiny bed-sit in a place called Wallasey, which is on the opposite side of the river from Liverpool. My parents were not impressed and the landlady kept switching off the gas and electricity at eight o'clock each evening, so we went to bed feeling hungry and that word 'unhappiness' was already creeping in to my mind.

We moved in with Eric's parents. They ran the largest pub in Liverpool which was called the Blue Ball Hotel. It was immensely popular, but not with my parents. Eric's mother, a broad blonde, pretty woman, though in a masculine sort of way, gave us a room which overlooked the police station yard next door, and for which we were very grateful, and we spent our first night listening to the police bringing the criminals into the yard immediately beneath our window. There was a lot of screaming and bad language, and underneath the room was the bar, with its singing, shouting and I heard words that I had never heard in my life before.

Eric finally found a flat for us in Aigburth – a rather posh part of Liverpool. It was a lovely flat and was owned by a very intelligent, rather professorial man. For the first time, I felt married. In fact, happily married. Eric was getting on very well in Harland & Wolfe and bliss seemed to be visiting us. There was one problem: my cooking. I cannot believe it now, but the first meal I gave to Eric in our idyllic niche was a sort of soup which on its own was OK, but in an effort to be creative I placed a little pork pie in the middle and it sank immediately, turning the whole dish into something truly bizarre. I must add at this point that I had not yet become a vegetarian, but it was travelling towards me.

It was in this flat that I became pregnant, the beginnings of which were not very pleasant. I spent my early mornings heaving in the bathroom and my afternoons being driven around by my frantic father, who was home from sea, in an effort to try and interest me in life. This went on for quite a long time and the excitement that I had felt that pregnancy might bring had now turned into some kind of nightmare. Instead of putting on weight, I lost weight. There was nothing on any menu that I could possibly stomach and my doctor grew sick and tired of me and stopped making suggestions.

Only moments after I wished I were dead, things suddenly turned. I awoke one morning feeling different. I travelled to the bathroom and put myself in the 'being sick' position, but nothing happened. I managed to eat some breakfast and instead of Eric rushing out to work trying to avoid the cry of 'I don't want this baby', he lingered and his parting was akin to any romantic scene I had seen or read about. From then on, I enjoyed the whole business. The fatter I grew, the prouder I became. I wandered about the large shops of Liverpool where many of my friends worked with no other intention than to make them jealous.

An abrupt end to this ecstasy came one evening at about nine o'clock. Eric was teaching at night school, so I called a taxi. I was in the very early stages of labour and I wandered into the Royal Liverpool Infirmary, which was where most babies were born in those days. It was a large, dark green, tiled, Victorian building with long corridors. There was no reception, so I went along the corridor and met my first nurse. 'Hello love,' she said, "av' yer gorra pain?' in her wonderful Liverpool accent. She led me to what was called the Labour Room. There were three beds in a row, side by side, two of them were occupied by women who seemed as if they were about to give birth to a breeze block. I was told to undress and lie on the third bed, which I did. After a few moments, a nurse came in and examined me and she wrote on a large blackboard at the end of my bed all the various dimensions of the most secret parts of my body, and then she disappeared. The lady next to me, a large blonde, said, 'Is this your first love?' I tried to say 'yes', but it came out in a sort of scream as I was gripped by a contraction.

'This is me seventh. I'll bloody kill him if he comes near me again.'

The lady in the other bed was now squawking on the highest note. A ward sister came in: 'Oh for goodness' sake, Mrs Wainwright, you've hardly started yet. Where's your gas and air? Have you dropped the mask again?' She tut-tutted and walked out.

During the next forty-eight hours that I spent in that same little prison, several ladies came in, had their babies and went out. I, on the other hand, was still heaving and pushing but to no avail. They kept giving me gas but it kept running out and by this time I hated Eric more than any other person or thing in the world. Finally, my first son was born. He made a great song and dance about it. I don't know how many people or nurses I psychologically harmed during my very vocal pleas for God to take me in that little Labour Room, but looking down at this little human being – perfect, bright eyed and making a meal of his little fist – all memories of pain and anguish fled. The Liverpool Royal Infirmary was demolished soon afterwards, and my younger son, Nigel, was born eighteen months later, in a more civilised manner in Broadgreen Hospital.

Chapter **2**

WASP & DADDY

When my children were babies in a pram, I used to take them through Sandfield Park in which stood an enormous Victorian building called Claremont House set in its own grounds. I was fascinated by it from the start. So much so that I had the nerve to push the pram up the long drive and walk round it, enchanted for reasons I couldn't understand. I did this several times and then Mrs Comer, who lived in the house and owned it, spotted me one day and sent her three dogs after me. I ended up legging it down the drive pushing my bewildered children and just managing to get through the big gate in time. Nevertheless, I always stood and stared at the house and never knew why. It held something for me that even now I can't explain.

I had joined the Liverpool Writers' Club. It was held in a room above a restaurant called The Rembrandt. In this rather inhospitable room, potential writers gathered together to read their efforts and to learn from the other more successful writers. It was there that I met Myra Taylor – a glamorous lady who was noticeable in every way. Her readings were dark and without hope, and I saw in her a potential lasting friendship. And some of my funniest moments were indeed spent with My, as I called her. She called me Ro – short for Romana – and although we didn't know it, we were going to make a journey into the celebrity world together.

I had begun to write short articles and had been selling them to local radio. The most successful one was called 'Love Me Love My Wasp'. It was triggered off when one day I walked into the lounge where my faithful cleaning lady, Mrs Duval, was working. I was just in time to see her run the vacuum cleaner over a wasp which was making a valiant attempt to cross the carpet. I was horrified and it must have shown on my face because she immediately switched off the Hoover and stared at me. 'How could you?' I exploded. 'How could you run the Hoover over an innocent, harmless little creature like that?' She stared at me in amazement.

'They sting,' she said.

'Only if you torment them,' I said.

She could see that I was truly upset by her action so she offered her 'mend all' sentence: 'Let's have a cup of tea.' During this particular tea break, in an effort to make me realise that not all creatures were kind, I suffered a long monologue concerning the rats in her back yard and her old man's method of destruction. She then proceeded to bring almost all living creatures into her excuse for killing the wasp. 'OK, OK,' I said, 'I'm calm now, I'm calm.'

When she had gone I rushed to the Hoover bag and emptied it onto some newspaper. And there it was – alive and well – a little blob of dust with legs. I brushed it down and set it on the floor and let it go into a dark corner to recover. I was so moved by this episode that I wrote this article and sent it to the local radio. They were really thrilled with it and wanted me to read it but, after hearing me, they very politely said, 'We have an experienced lady who will read it.' I can only imagine that my Liverpool accent, although it was mild, was not 'posh' enough for the BBC in those days.

One day, as I was hanging out some clothes in the garden, a face peered at me through the hedge. It was my father, and I immediately noticed how very blue his eyes were. 'I need to talk to you,' he said quietly. All kinds of things crossed my mind as I opened the front door and prepared cups of coffee. He seemed to have difficulty getting his words together. 'I'm ill,' he said.

My stomach turned over. 'Ill, what kind of ill, Daddy?'

'It's my heart. I've had several warnings. Don't tell your mother. I just wanted you to know.' And again he said, 'Please don't tell Hive' – his name for my mother, whose real name was Ivy Amelia.

It was hard for me to keep this secret. Of course, in those days there was no real way of dealing with my father's problem. If he had lived a few years longer he would have been rescued by today's knowledge and technology.

Only a few weeks later, my mother rang me. 'Come quickly,' she said, 'your father's ill.' He was lying in bed, fully clothed, with a blanket over him. His lovely face was grey and there seemed to be no difference between the colour of his skin and the faint little bits of silver in his dark hair. My mother was in the lounge wringing her hands and unable to face the situation. Marna was crying in another bedroom and Daddy kept saying 'Don't call a doctor, please don't call an ambulance, please don't call anything.'

He was rambling, but all his ramblings were saying the same thing: he wanted to die at home. I tried to make him comfortable but it was impossible. He was tossing and turning and clutching at his chest. 'Daddy,' I said, 'I must call an ambulance.' For a moment it looked as though all the pain had gone and he stared at me, saying, 'No, no'. The telephone was right beside the bed and I decided to try and smuggle it out of the door and into the hall, but he saw my intentions and his 'no's' became more desperate.

'All right,' I said, 'all right. I'll get you some water.' And I ran into the lounge and told my mother that I was going to the phone box, which was only five minutes away. She didn't answer; she was just staring through the window.

They had met when she was seventeen and he was eighteen. It was obvious that they loved each other and it was the one thing that formed the wonderful umbrella of safety over us when we were children. I phoned for an ambulance and ran back to the house. As I walked into the bedroom, Daddy looked at me and he knew I had betrayed him. I sat on the edge of the bed, stroking his hair and massaging his hands. Within a very short time, there was a knock at the door and quite clearly you could hear my mother saying 'This way, he's upstairs.' Daddy looked at me and whispered, 'I'll never forgive you.'

He died moments later, before they were able to put him on the stretcher. Speaking to the specialist a few days later, he said to me, 'I told your father to remember the saying "My life is in the hands of those who choose to anger me".' To this day, I feel that I was the one to anger him.

Chapter 3

FROM PEN TO SCREEN

One day, as Myra and I were sitting in the Adelphi Hotel having coffee and swapping mundane news, we talked about television and the things we liked to watch. *Monty Python* came up as a favourite, and our excitement grew so much that we decided to try and write something. The first thing we wrote was called *Up Down and All Around*. It was a bizarre piece beginning with a dachshund dog being interviewed. He was complaining about the height of the pavements and that his anatomy was such that they needed to be lower. We sent this to the Head of Comedy at the BBC. We didn't expect anything to come of it, but one day, while I was sitting in my house, my phone rang. It was the Head of Comedy and he asked if we could go and see him.

Eric sat without any sign of emotion as with great excitement I related this phone call. I wanted him to pick me up and swing me round the way he often did, shouting, 'Well done, darling, well done', but I realised that he was afraid. And the joy of this news was diluted. He did however run me to the station and seemed much brighter.

'Enjoy yourself darling,' he said.

And Myra and I ran to the waiting train. Myra's husband Hal sat, white faced, in his car.

'I'm sorry I'm late,' said My, 'but I had to show him how to warm his dinner up.'

We sat on the London train in disbelief, which was partnered by fear. Myra said, 'Where is the Television Centre, anyway?'

'I haven't a clue,' I said.

Myra asked, 'Are you sure it was the Head of Comedy?'

My heart missed a beat.

'Of course I am. It was Michael Mills.'

She said, 'I've never heard of him.'

'Neither have I, but his secretary spoke to me.'

'Are you sure?'

Suddenly I was not sure, and the whole journey was clouded with uncertainty.

It was strange as we walked along the main corridor leading to the Head of Comedy's office. He was a short, sturdy man with a large beard and he wore white socks. He was not quite the kind of man one expected to see. He fired his questions straight between the eyes and his observations were not cloaked in niceties.

'This,' he thundered, tapping our manuscript with a pen, 'this is funny but not many people would understand it.'

We were too frightened to argue. He swung around in his black leather chair. 'Do you live together?'

'No, no,' we chorused. 'We're both married.'

'I see.'

He tapped his pen against an inkwell. 'Could you write about two women who did live together?' He could see our inability to imagine what kind of a relationship he was talking about. 'Say, two girls, young girls,' he emphasised, 'sharing a bed-sit, or a flat, if you like.'

We left the Television Centre with a commission to write a series about two young girls sharing a bed-sit or a flat if you like. We sat in the taxi and hardly spoke. We got on the train and hardly spoke. We ordered sandwiches but could not eat them. We ordered tea but could not drink it. Then Myra said, 'Christ Ro, we've been commissioned to write a series.'

'I know, I know,' I heard myself saying.

'Hal will have a bloody fit,' she said, 'going to London every five minutes.'

'I don't think Eric will be all that pleased,' I said.

'Jesus,' she said.

'Jesus,' I said.

The train was going through the wet, black tunnel which brought us into Lime Street Station. We babbled as we parted. 'I'll talk to you tomorrow,' said Myra.

'OK.' I said, and I called after her, 'We'll do it, we'll do it.'

Chapter 4

FAMILY

Carl and Nigel were now nine and eleven. A time of discovery, a time of wanting to go to the baths, to go off on their bicycles, to be free of constant discipline, not a time for me to be planning to be away from home. When Eric dropped me off at the Adelphi, which is where we continued to do our writing, his face was frozen with disapproval.

'Who's going to take care of the children?' he asked.

'Mrs Duval – I've arranged it,' I said.

'She is a cleaner,' he said, 'is she going to put them to bed?'

'No, you are.'

'I go to my club on Mondays and Fridays.'

'Then I'll try to be home on those days.'

'What happens if you are asked to write more . . .?'

'If we are asked to write more, Eric, we will write more. It's what I've always wanted to do. You know that. The children will be cared for, I will see to it. In fact, they will benefit by it.' My voice took on a soprano leap. 'It's money!'

'I can earn all the money we need.'

'But what about me, I need to do something important.'

Clouds were gathering.

'Being my wife is important.' I never realised that Eric could possibly think like this.

'You are important, for God's sake. You are my husband.' And I found myself wishing he wasn't.

The waiters in the Adelphi Hotel were used to Myra and me having coffee regularly and they were very impressed with our news. They came and went with free sandwiches and extra coffee, and the little chap who wandered round holding up a board with chalk messages on it, visited our corner of the big lounge often. One morning the board read: 'Phone call for Carla Lane or Myra Taylor.' We leapt up and rushed to the reception desk. 'Excuse me, did someone leave a message?'

'No Madam.'

'Did they say who they were?'

'No Madam.'

'A number?'

'No Madam.'

We went back to our seats.

'It's probably the BBC,' I said.

'It's probably Hal,' Myra said.

We started to discuss the characters. We called them Beryl and Sandra. One posh and one not so posh, and they would indeed share a flat together. We decided that Sandra's mother, now divorced, would be pretentious, and that Beryl's mother, living miserably with her husband, would be very ordinary – common perhaps.

Outside the hotel that evening, Eric sat in his car and it was obvious he was angry and, as Myra and I were saying goodbye to each other, I could also see that Hal was in a state of 'who's going to get my dinner?' Before I had got one leg into our car, Eric told me he had spent most of the afternoon with the police after our sons Carl and Nigel were seen taking a short cut in the local park by riding their bicycles through the flower beds.

'Why, why would they do that?' I wailed.

Eric fired his first arrow: 'They need someone to discipline them.'

They stood before me, fresh faced and a little scared. I asked the question again, 'Why would you do such a thing?' Eric was watching racing on television. 'Why!' I shrieked. Eric turned the sound up. We shuffled out into the breakfast room. I plonked each one on a chair and tried to control my voice, which had taken on a Maria Callas-like sound. 'I mean, I mean, why? Your father is a busy, hard-working man. He didn't want to be called away from his work by the police, because his sons were running amok among the dahlias – dahlias for goodness' sake.' There was a long, long silence. 'Well, you weren't here,' said Carl quietly. Oh God, I thought, it's started already – you weren't here – how often was I going to hear that.

That night Eric and I lay in bed, we had had good sex and we spoke lovingly. Eric asked, 'Can Mrs Duval cook?'

I replied, 'Better than I can.' He sighed and ruffled my hair.

'It's not even definite Eric, yet,' I said. 'It's a trial; they may not like what we do – I love you, will that do for now?'

He laughed long and noisily. 'What?' I said. 'What?'

'You're writing it already,' he said, and we slept peacefully.

The following day I spent with my mother. We were sitting in the grounds of an old Victorian house. It had been empty for a long time and it was a pleasant and safe place for the children to run and ride their bicycles. My mother loved Eric and I found myself confiding that he was sometimes not the person I wanted him to be. Looking at me with her darker than brown eyes she said, 'I'm damn sure you're not the person he wants you to be. All those trips to London.'

I was raising my voice again, 'Twice, that's all, twice.'

'And more to come,' she said.

'It was different for you,' I said. 'Daddy was away all the time. It keeps the romance alive. I find it hard to please a husband and myself too.'

My mother sighed, 'All I'm saying is, don't let all this BBC stuff go to your head. If you don't get it right, see if they care.'

Chapter 5

PADDINGTON

The BBC was anxious to see what we had written. Mr Mills asked us to send a manuscript. We were about to do that when he made a second call.

'I think you should come to London. I want you to meet the producer,' he said, quickly adding, 'is it funny this script, is it funny?'

'Yes, yes,' we chorused.

'When can you come to London?'

'We need a few days.'

'I'm arranging a meeting here.'

I cupped the phone and said to Myra, 'He's arranging a meeting in London.'

'Oh shit,' said Myra.

'Let me see, Thursday, we'll come on Thursday.'

Myra was vigorously shaking her head and mouthing, 'No, no'.

'Eleven thirty, yes, yes, fine. Thank you.'

I put the phone down. 'I can't go then,' said Myra. 'It's Hal's day off.'

'We've got to go, Myra; it's all part of it.'

'Oh shit,' she said again.

'I know, oh shit,' I said.

Eric dropped Myra and me off at Lime Street Station. 'Be careful darling,' he called as we rushed towards the departing train. I turned and waved and threw a kiss. He stood on the platform for a few moments, smiling that brave smile which I dreaded so much. Myra had already said goodbye to Hal. She had tears in her eyes. Once on the train, I opened the window and waved both arms until my life was threatened by an approaching bridge.

'Oh, for God's sake,' said Myra, 'why are you so bloody lucky? My fella went into a coma when I told him I had to go to London again, my daughter cried and the bloody cat was sick.' She laughed the way she always did, an uninhibited chesty laugh, followed by the words, 'Where are my fags?' She foraged into the depths of her bottomless handbag and in a moment was deeply inhaling nicotine and throwing out a grey-blue stream of smoke. 'That's better,' she said.

Later she would go for yet another coffee and I used to watch her coming along the aisle, tight, tight sweater, boasting noticeable breasts, a wide, red-lipstick smile, green eyes, decorated with black mascara, black liner and black eye shadow. Men looked up from their newspapers as she passed and she rewarded each one with an extra thrust of her chest.

I whispered to her as she sat down, 'You are a tart.'

'I know,' she said, 'aren't you jealous?'

The BBC office was crowded. Pauline Collins and Polly James, the two girls who were to play the parts of Beryl and Sandra were there. They seemed shy and not at all loud and confident, the way I had imagined actresses to be. Michael Mills was chatting to potential directors of the show but he waved to us as we walked in, trying to look as if we had done it all before so many times. Myra had already clapped her eyes on a red-haired chap, tall and smiling. I knew because her legs took up the pursuing position – they were crossed in a way that nobody could hold for more than a few minutes, sort of crossed but not quite crossed so as not to make her calves look fat.

Eventually, Michael Mills called order and explained that he was holding up the meeting until the producer arrived. 'However,' he said, 'you have all got copies of the manuscript and apart from minor changes

I think we have already agreed that it is workable. Perhaps a little more of the parents of these two girls would enhance it.'

There followed a discussion about the technical details of the show, where in Liverpool we might film and Pauline asked whether or not she was to be very posh or a little posh, and Polly said, 'I'm dead common, I'm fine with that.' We touched on the subject of wardrobe and how the flat might look, and we bandied a few more names of people who might play other parts. Finally, the wonderful Mollie Sugden, who was very much a favourite for the part of Mrs Hutchinson suggested that we all go and have a cup of tea.

That evening, Myra and I sat in our room in Paddington and read the script. I played Sandra and she played Beryl. We couldn't stop laughing all the way through and we felt really pleased. 'It's smashing,' I said. 'Bloody brilliant,' said Myra.

There was a knock on the door. It was Mr Abbot, the owner of the bed and breakfast – 'Are you two girls all right then? There's tea and stuff in the basement, toast if you want it,' he said in his 'I'm Welsh and proud of it' way. He left before we could answer.

'I like him,' I said.

'He's Welsh,' said Myra.

'So?'

'They sing a lot.'

I curled up laughing. It was nerves really.

'What on earth does that mean?'

'They're always singing,' she said, 'about the hills and the sheep and everything else that's Welsh.'

'My grandma was Welsh,' I said, 'and she didn't even like hills or sheep, for God's sake.'

We were both laughing now.

'She was lying,' said Myra.

And so the conversation went on until we were both holding our stomachs, an obvious attack of nerves tinged with terror.

Finally, I said, 'Did you meet the producer?'

'No,' said Myra, 'I was talking to a fella called Alan.'

'Yes, I noticed.'

'OK, OK, so I'm sexy and beautiful. What's wrong with that?'

Later, very awake and thoughtful, with Myra making strange little noises in her sleep at the other end of the room, I felt a mixture of excitement and dread. We had hardly touched the world of television and yet I knew I could never go back to just being Mrs Hollins. Guilt visited me now so I got up quietly and went to the phone box at the end of the hall and rang Eric.

'He's not in,' said Mrs Duval, 'he's at the Conservative Club.'

'Oh fine,' I said, 'and the boys – are they OK?'

'They're watching *Danger Man*,' she said.

'Oh good, give them my love.'

'I will, yeah.'

'I'll be home tomorrow.'

'OK, tarra.'

I put the phone down and in my head I went over her words. 'He's at the club . . . they're watching *Danger Man*.' Now I would sleep. As I came out of the phone box, a naked man opened the door of his room and quickly shut it again. 'How funny it all is down here,' I thought. Where was he going? Why didn't he have any clothes on? I fell asleep without an answer.

Chapter **6**

WINGS & THINGS

I didn't know it at the time but Michael Mills was not very impressed with our script. It hadn't worked the way he had expected and he had invited two other men to write the rest. They were introduced to us as 'helpers' because we were new writers. Both men were older than we were and full of confidence. We sat in a BBC office together thinking out another storyline. Myra and I joined forces and spoke about Sandra's proper upbringing and Beryl's rather common parents. But they had different ideas altogether and went for jokes instead of reality. Not that our script had much reality in it. Nervous of not being funny, we had left out the thoughtful bits but it was obvious that we were on completely different wavelengths. Eric had a mild attack of displeasure when I told him I couldn't get home; Hal was furious with Myra.

'I'll have to go Ro,' she said, 'he wants his bloody dinner.'

'But My, I can't cope by myself,' I said. 'Not now, not yet. Can't you ring him again?'

She left quietly dragging her enormous suitcases behind her and taking ages to get it and herself into the taxi. I waved her off and my stomach was doing somersaults. I heard the phone ringing inside. I ran to it.

'Hello.'

'Hello.' It was the producer. 'Are you all right you two?'

'Er, yes, yes. Well, Myra has had to go home but I'll . . .'

'How did you get on with the new writers?'

I wanted to cry. It sounded so final, so finished. 'Oh fine, yes, we'll get something together.'

'Have you eaten?'

'Er, yes, no, well I'm about to.'

'I'll leave you then. See you in the office tomorrow.'

'Yes, yes, bye.'

It was a lonely time sitting in that room, watching the grey light of day turn to the yellow light of night. Paddington was a big and exciting place, but for me, on my own, there was nowhere to go. Loneliness gathered and ruled out the joy of being a television writer – I wanted to go home.

The BBC finally decided to put out three of our scripts out and that the two other writers would write the other three. Disappointing though that was, the series became a hit right away. The next morning reporters gathered in the corridors outside the producer's office at the BBC. The ratings had been amazing – Myra and I were inside the office coping with the first batch of reporters. We were perched on a desk, our mini skirts made modesty impossible. 'Look up,' they shouted. We looked up. 'Now look down.' We looked down. 'Now turn this way.' We turned that way. 'Lean forwards.' We leaned forwards. 'A little more, that's better. A bit more.' The cameras were clicking, lights flashing. We were full of joy. So this was television, this was fame.

A voice interrupted my thoughts. 'Could you just undo that top button?' We undid the top button. And when they got to the 'now look down' again, it was as if the same thought entered both our minds at the same moment. We sat up and buttoned our top button again. There was something wrong with how it was going. Some of the men were on their knees. We called it a day and made an excuse to go for breakfast.

Back at Mr Abbot's he greeted us waving the evening newspaper. 'There's more downstairs on the table,' he said. 'The chap next door picked this one up. I've had all sorts of people here, but I've never had anyone famous before.'

My eyes rested on the first page of one of the papers – the headline said: 'The Liver Birds from Liverpool' and I froze as I looked at the picture. We had both leaned so far forward that our cleavages were the only things you could concentrate on. In a smaller picture, we were both looking up as requested, so up that we looked as though we had some kind of brain damage. Myra was wearing her well-practised, sexy smile but I looked as if I was deformed. Mr Abbot plonked a pot of tea and a mountain of toast on the table. 'Oh, by the way,' he said, 'a chap rang last night – I didn't get his name – he said he was the producer of the show – a well spoken chap he was, a bit BBCish. He said he popped into the office yesterday to keep an eye on you both, but you were coping very well and he'd see you at the next rehearsal.' I wanted to hide, or go home, or disintegrate.

Chapter 7

NEW HEIGHTS

The series ran for six weeks. It created much excitement and good press. Hal loved it, Eric thought it was all right. The producer ran us to Euston Station on the last night. 'So,' he said, 'we'll wait and see now.'

'Yes,' I said.

'Yes,' said Myra.

'It's done very well,' he said, 'top ratings.'

'Yes.'

'Yes.'

How mysterious this man was. No one seemed to know anything about him. He hadn't been married, he didn't seem to have a woman in his life. He lived alone in a Chiswick flat and loved classical music.

'He's gay,' said Myra.

And then it came, the phone call. Michael Mills wanted to know if Myra and I could write another series.

'*The Liver Birds*,' he said, 'have done very well.' Although he would have liked a little less frivolity, a little less cliché in the plots and a lot more real life.

I phoned Myra immediately. I babbled the message to her – she muttered something typically Myra which was: 'Hal and I are standing on a rock in the middle of an emotional sea and I'm waiting to see who is going to jump first.'

I babbled excitedly, 'Oh come on, My,' I said, 'we've got enough real life going on between us to write another twenty series.'

'How much are they paying us? I might be able to persuade him.'

'Well obviously more,' I said.

'I'll ring you back. His car is about to explode, so we might be lucky.'

We were on the train the next day, this time it was first class, courtesy of the BBC.

People were staring at us again – I could hear the whispers, 'There's those two *Liver Birds* women.' I would get my mirror out to see if my face had suffered an upheaval and as usual, Myra would present her tight-sweatered chest. The tables were set for breakfast; it was all orange and deep blue. The waiter who had already noticed Myra took an order for coffee and sandwiches. I requested vegetarian and Myra said, 'You can put a bullock in mine, if you like.' He could not take his eye off her variety of pouts. When he had gone I said, 'How do you do it, My? How do you bowl all these men over?'

'You're lucky Ro. Men don't admit fancying you – you sit there with your cold stare.'

'Cold stare.'

'Well it's hardly come and get me, is it? With your pale makeup and your daft blonde hair.'

'Daft, why daft?'

'Well, it's not bossed about, is it – it does what it likes.'

I secretly thought that I would much rather have her thick, dark hair.

'And your pale pink gob!'

She mimicked, 'Keep away from me, I'm inhibited.' With me,' she said, 'what you see is what you get.'

'And what they see is a tart.'

We both laughed.

The waiter had brought our coffee and she had caught his attention like an angler catches his fish in an inescapable net, but she decided to fall asleep. Her closed eyes with their charcoal eye shadow and black eyelashes suddenly looked like sleeping spiders.

I wasn't tired and I loved the train: the different kinds of landscape rising and merging, green fields dotted with sheep, grey-tiled roof tops, tiny gardens cluttered with tiny greenhouses, old sheds, little plants in little pots, tired privets, deckchairs, old prams, old bricks, bins, washing, kids' tricycles, swings, pet rabbits and bits of motorbike. It was during these journeys that perhaps I thought I was a writer. I thought very much of my grandfather. All I had to do was put into sentences the things I saw and felt.

And so it was all starting again – the excitement, the worry and also in my chest a pleasant little pain at the thought of seeing 'Him' again.

Chapter 8

THE ARRIVAL OF SUCCESS

Mr Abbot was standing on the steps of his bed and breakfast. He waved and smiled as we fell out of the taxi and he raised his eyes to heaven when he saw the usual endless luggage – cases, big bags, little bags, boxes, umbrellas – as he once described our luggage in his lovely Welsh accent, 'a taxi full of bloody frocks'.

Our room was unchanged, but Myra had brought a curtain that she was going to hang across the corner where the basin was.

'This,' she said, 'is to promote modesty. I don't know what deformities you have, but you won't have to camp out beneath a bath towel at wash time.'

Soon, she was banging away with a rather stoic ashtray and our modesty curtain was hung. The usual rose, packed in my case by Eric, took up its place on the little table by my bed and as usual Myra's table was littered with fags, as she called them.

'Oh God,' I moaned, 'soon we'll be fogged out again. I'll have to sleep with my nightie over my head.'

Mr Abbot brought us a pot of tea and some biscuits and, having noticed my passion for animals, he also deposited a tiny stray cat on the sofa.

'I've no idea where he came from, sitting on the step he was and still here this morning. I can't have him downstairs. The guests wouldn't like it, see. Cheeky little bugger he is; takes the toast out of their mouths he does.'

'Ah,' cooed Myra.

I gathered the kitten up and Mr Abbot vanished before we changed our minds. This little cat took up residence with Mr Abbot and moved in with me whenever I went to stay there.

The producer, now referred to as "Him" was still casting when we arrived at the BBC. We were shown to the small bar to wait. Since Pauline Collins, who played Sandra, had left for a bigger part in another show, the producer was now searching for someone new. It was such a strange situation – we two in the BBC, surrounded by all the people we usually saw on the television. Particularly, as it was a Wednesday and in those days all the pop stars used to arrive on that day.

We ordered a glass of lemonade each, just to prove how worldly we were and we watched all these famous faces. Bruce Forsyth was the first one we spotted – he was with some friends and in spite of the attention he had to give them, he smiled at us and said, 'Oh I say, new faces.' We of course smiled back and a couple of Pan's People wandered in. They were very beautiful and knew it. And there were a good deal of girly giggles as they ordered and paid for their drinks. At the main door was a desk and sitting behind it, an Irishman. He had to take down everyone's name and enter it in a book. He also had to answer the masses of incoming calls and then page the person concerned. In his lovely Irish voice, he would say 'Would Sir John Geilgud please come to the phone?' 'Would Mr Ronnie Barker please come to the phone?' 'Would Miss Judi Dench please come to the phone?' It was all so bewildering. Captain Mainwaring strolled by, he tipped his forehead as if he were in *Dad's Army* and smiled at us.

Somehow or other, Myra had moved from our table and was in a corner talking and laughing with Dennis Main Wilson, a well-loved producer. My loneliness was staved off by the producer who came into the bar with Nerys Hughes. She and Sir John Geilgud hugged each other and I found myself in their company. I had never seen this man before and, as the little crowd around me grew, we were drawn together in conversation. Overwhelmed and not knowing what to say, I came out with 'And what do you do?'

He looked down at me and in his charming, unruffled voice, replied, 'I act a little. What do you do?'

'I write *The Liver Birds*,' I said with pride.

At this point the producer joined us again and greeted him. 'Sir John,' he said, 'how are you for goodness' sake? I haven't seen you for ages.'

'Oh, I've been here and there,' he replied with great modesty.

I think at that moment I experienced the loneliest two minutes of my life, and was saved from rushing out through the door by the producer who introduced me to Nerys, a lovely and charming person, who knew all the girly tricks which drew everybody towards her and, although this did nothing to give me the confidence I needed, I was delighted that she was to play the part of Sandra.

I was even more pleased that we had not lost Michael Angelis, who played the part of Lucien. My favourite Scouser, Michael is a warm hearted man – he played his part exactly the way I saw it, which was exactly the way he saw it, which is unusual. He didn't have to do funny things to make people laugh, he just had to sit there and sing the words to his own tune, and it always came out right, and in the business of comedy, 'right' had to be funny. Michael was able to bring much of his own compassion into the lines given him – he knew exactly when to make you laugh and exactly when to make you cry. Playing the part of Lucien, who had a passionate love for his rabbits, was perfect because one actually got the impression that he was passionate about rabbits. And the bonus was that he became one of my best mates.

'Where was Myra?' you are asking. Well, she was in the corner of the small bar, entertaining an entire pop group and even though they were younger than she, they were obviously hooked on her. Each time they asked her a question, she would raise her green eyes at the ceiling and purse her very red lips. It never failed.

Nerys was pleased with the role of Sandra. We discussed various little nuances concerning her character. She liked the idea of being the snob and of Beryl being down to earth. She also wanted to be just a little naïve compared with Beryl. 'I think,' she said, 'that Beryl is much more earthy than Sandra, much more rough if you like, whereas Sandra is sweet and trusting.' She hesitated and said in fun, 'And boring.' We all laughed.

Myra and I had already decided these things and they were evident in the series which we had already written. The producer was captivated by Nerys, and we eventually left them to cope with the masses of people who embraced them, kissed them and praised them. 'They'll be doing that to us soon,' I said.

'Oh, yeah,' said Myra. 'as they're showing us the way to the bloody station.'

That night the phone rang in the hall at Abbot's. Mr Abbot knocked on our door and peeped round. 'Some chap – it's for you Carla,' he said.

'Oh, it'll be Eric,' I thought as I plodded to the phone.

'Have I called at the wrong time?' It was 'Him'.

'No, no, we're just messing about.'

'So what do you think about Nerys as Sandra?'

'She's just right,' I said. 'Both Myra and I agree on that.'

'Oh good, I think that too. I've admired her in other shows.'

There was a long pause; neither of us seemed to know how to carry on the conversation.

'Does Polly know?' I eventually asked.

'Oh yes, she's fine with it.'

Longer pause. 'Have you eaten, you two?'

He always asked that question.

'Er, yes, well no, but we're too anxious to go out so we've had a sandwich here.'

'Oh,' he said, 'all right. I suppose the next thing is a script.'

'Yes, we'll do it as fast as we can. The schedule seems rather harsh.'

'All right then. Oh, when are you going back to Liverpool?'

'Er, tomorrow, yes tomorrow.'

'All right, I'll, er, I'll see you.'

'Yes.'

'Bye.'

'Bye.'

I stood in the phone booth for a second or two. One part of me was denying it, but the other part of me was shouting very loudly that these silly, meaningless conversations were beginning to excite me.

I went back to Myra. She was behind the makeshift curtain that she had draped round the wash basin. 'What did he want?' she said through vigorous brushing of teeth.

'Oh, just to see if we were OK.'

'And are we?'

'Yes, aren't we?'

She came out in her dressing gown, still brushing her teeth.

'Carla,' she said through the foam, 'I need to talk to you, OK?'

'OK'

'I'm not pulling my weight, am I?'

'I don't know what you mean.'

'Oh come on, Carla, you know very well. You write the scripts, you, not me, not me.'

'Rubbish.'

'No, I'm serious. I'm backing out.'

I felt sick inside.

'Oh come on Myra.'

'This is not for me; you know what I'm like. I want to write black, heart-twisting, gritty stuff. You always called me the drama queen. Well, you're right. I can't write funny scripts.'

'Then we'll write funny, black, drama scripts.'

'No, I'm serious, I'm not coming back to London.'

'But we've had a great time, Myra. Is it me, have I done something?'

'Apart from being right every time, no.'

She was near to tears.

'It's just that I don't feel able to cope with another series. What with Hal screaming at me all the time to come home and my daughter misses me. She's twelve years old, she needs me around and besides, you're the writer, not me.'

'Rubbish,' I kept saying, 'rubbish.'

The conversation went on for a long time, long enough for Myra to have mowed her way through half a tube of toothpaste. Finally, we fell silent.

I lay there in the familiar shadowy light, listening to a crowd of drunks laughing outside our bed and breakfast hotel. Now and then the phone rang in the hall and I kept wishing it were someone who could comfort me. Nothing would be the same. Coming to London on my own held no delight. I could hear the little sleeping noises coming from her end of the room. I knew I would never enjoy a friend as much as I enjoyed Myra. And worse, I wasn't sure if I could write without her.

It was a black journey home. Neither of us knew what to say to each other. I pointed to a large dying tree in the middle of a field. It was being strangled by ivy.

'Like me,' said Myra.

I was going to delve deeply into the nonsense of her remark but she was already causing the man with the sandwich trolley to get his tea mixed up with his coffee and drop several packets of biscuits, so I kept silent.

Chapter 9

ANOTHER HILL TO CLIMB

During the time between the first series of *The Liver Birds* and the third, Claremont House had come up for sale. I had money now and what better way to spend it. Mrs Comer, the owner, was glad to sell it to me, and the entire family moved in – my mother, my two sons, Eric and me, our dogs, our parrots – and each of us had a private and lovely place of our own within the house.

Claremont House was huge; it had approximately forty rooms and two huge spiral staircases, one at each end of a long, long hall. Outside there was a courtyard with stables, which were very old now, a large lawn, an orchard and other grounds surrounding the house. It fronted onto a quiet road on the edge of Sandfield Park. It was after I had moved the last items of furniture into this wonderful place that I walked silently round it. Without doubt, we had an affinity, the house and I. I am certain that it beckoned me. The place I loved most to sit and write was on the bank of the old, old railway that ran along one side of this house. It was set in a deep well of red sandstone, just a single line, ferns and coloured bushes grew among the stones. Now and then an old train would pass through. I never knew where it came from or where it was going. The rest of my work on *The Liver Birds* would, during the summer, be written on the wide bank at the top of this old railway where birds sang and the old house crouched over me.

My favourite place in the house was the old kitchen. It, like the staircases, was set off the main hall, but there were five steps down to it. It had a red-tiled floor and old, tiled walls. In this kitchen many, many sad and beautiful things were going to happen during our stay there.

Eric was very happy living in Claremont. We had a sizeable flat overlooking the front lawns and my mother's part of the house joined us. The only thing he could never quite come to terms with was the fact that I had bought the house and I couldn't make him understand that it was the best, best thing that I could have done.

It was round about this time that I realised that while I had loved Eric so much in our youth and during the time our children were born, I had now come to feel less close to him. I could not criticise him in any way. He was always immaculate, he walked straight and with pride, no longer the gangling youth I married. He was a good man, he worked hard, he looked after us and he was generous. He was also a gambler, which sometimes caused huge hiccups in the family budget but never quite ruined it. I admired his dignity and I would always love his wry smile but I no longer had that actual 'being in love' feeling. I kept trying to pull it all back, but it was like trying to haul a great truck with a piece of string. I remember clearly those days and the emotional ache they caused.

Coming uninvited into my mind was 'Him'. Little darts of excitement accompanied these thoughts. I had tried hard to be what I was supposed to be, but the one thing I was successful at was being my mother's daughter. My happiest times in Claremont were with her. She was over sixty now but still beautiful with her almost black eyes and her still black hair. She fitted in with the comings and goings of my sons and their friends. She adored Eric. We spent a lot of time together, walking Egor the Wolfhound, going to Liverpool market, having tea in the Adelphi and, most of all, laughing. I can see now, the way she always covered her face with her young-looking hand when she laughed, and one day I captured a moment when I could talk to her about my growing confusion.

'I don't want to be married,' I said. 'I don't want the emotional rope that keeps pulling me back. I can't bear Eric's sad face.'

And the fact that it was obvious that Carl and Nigel knew exactly what was happening made me feel that I was letting down everybody I loved most, and if a friend of mine had come to me and said all these things just because she had tasted a different life, I would have told her how selfish she had become. My mother was listening intently.

'You see mother,' I said, 'I'm not sure who I actually am anymore.'

'You'll have to speak up,' she said, 'my hearing's going.'

The next day I took her to have her hearing tested. We came home and she was clutching a little box. We both spent ages trying to fit it into her ear and worse than that, whenever she removed it she could never remember where she'd left it.

'Where did you put it then?'

'In the little dish.'

'Which little dish? There are thousands of little dishes.'

'The one on the table by my chair.'

'It's not there – where is it now?'

'The cat must have knocked it down.'

So we grovelled around on the carpet, feeling with our hands.

'I need a plain carpet,' she said. 'You can't see it amongst all these colours.'

I was shouting now. 'OK, OK, so if we've lost it, we'll get another hearing aid, and in the meantime we'll get another carpet, OK?'

Although I felt angry, just looking at her face always made me smile and eventually laugh.

Eric and I had started going out in the car together, looking for little out of the way places in which to walk or eat. Egor, of course, came too, and he made the exercise enjoyable. There were moments when I watched Eric run along a little beach with Egor leaping about beside him that I felt as if I could drift back to being happy again. We would stop and kiss beside the sandstone rocks and something of the old feeling would ebb and flow for a while, but there was that word sex which held me back. I no longer seemed to need it – I had lost that little pulse which used to dart about inside me when I thought about it. Going to bed was a ritual. I lingered in the bathroom and no longer walked naked to the bed. I was encased in a Victorian nightie that I had bought in the market. It was too long so I kept tripping. It was too wide so I almost disappeared within it, and the journey from the bathroom to the marital bed became a comedy of errors. Finally, I landed, yards of Victorian cotton holding me safe from any intrusion. Eric would sit against a number of pillows, pretending to be reading, with his impressive chest bare. Once, I used to run my hands across it, but I pulled the bedclothes so high around me that his chest was now entombed.

They must have been sad, demoralising days for Eric, but he was too proud, or was it too clever, to show it. I would yawn rather like a mating seal and tuning in to the warning bell, Eric would stroke my hair briefly and say 'Night, God bless', and I would lie in the dark hating myself as I do now when recalling these moments.

Chapter 10

DOWNFALL

During the following days I managed to cause chaos by becoming ill, not ordinary ill but *very* ill, with a collection of weird symptoms which for a time baffled everybody, including the doctor, who announced that I had flu.

It had all begun with a headache and a temperature, so I settled down in bed waiting for it all to pass, but instead it became worse. The headache became a head pain and to my horror I woke up one morning and discovered that I could hardly see. Eric called the doctor in great panic. 'I think she's got polio,' he said.

So I was rushed to hospital with a police escort. It turned out that I had meningitis – every day at precisely one o'clock I was subjected to a lumbar puncture and the only thing that made the sound of that trolley coming towards me acceptable was the fact that the young doctor who was about to administer it was attractive and charming and sympathetic, and he got me through it by comforting me with little jokes.

I was in hospital for eleven weeks. Although I had been extremely ill, within a week of the illness I began to feel better – often many top medical men stood round my bed asking me questions and I seemed to have become a very interesting medical subject. Soon I was up and about making tea for everybody and desperately wanting to go home. My real disappointment was that I never heard from 'Him'. No phone call, no enquiry, nothing. I comforted myself with the thought that he was probably away filming some other show, as he often was. I then comforted myself more so by thinking that he probably was thinking about me, wondering where I was and probably desperate to see me again, but I was wrong – he was on holiday with his secretary.

After my recovery there followed a few weeks of normal family life. We all gathered in Claremont House – they were beautiful days. I was well recovered now, and my sons were happy with their lives. I spent much of my time wandering in the grounds of Claremont with my well-loved dog and sitting in the summerhouse talking to my mother. She was so funny, she didn't realise how funny she was. No matter what was happening in my life, my mother was always able to make me laugh.

Eric had been made redundant, as the ship building industry moved from Liverpool to Belfast. He pleaded with me to go with him but I had no interest in living in Belfast, especially as it was rather like a war zone there at the time. Although he was disappointed, a new idea visited him. He persuaded our sons, Carl and Nigel, now sixteen and seventeen, to open up a hairdressing salon of their own. They had both served an apprenticeship with Vidal Sassoon's salon and it seemed a really good idea. We also decided that my mother could be the receptionist. This excited her and borne on the wave of this unanimous family joy, I took her on holiday to Rome.

They were exciting days – I fell in love with Rome immediately and I towed her from art gallery to art gallery, day in and day out. 'I'm not into this art stuff,' she would say. 'Can't we go to another café?' And so it was café to café, gallery to gallery and, as we stood one day in the Pantheon, gazing at the statue of Christ in the arms of Our Lady, my mother's voice rang out, 'That is ridiculous – she couldn't possibly hold him like that – he'd fall through her knees.' There was a slight shuffle among everybody and I clutched her sleeve and marched her out.

We moved on to an exhibition of van Gogh's work. She had definite opinions about his work – 'I could do better than that when I was ten,' she said. 'Mother,' I said, 'please keep your thoughts to yourself – we'll talk about them when we get back to the hotel.' I dearly wanted to go once again to Florence and see the statue of David but I if I did I knew that I would have to leave my mother at home as she would only, in her noticeable voice, pass comment about his genitalia.

One day, as we were crossing the road to go back to the hotel, a motorbike came tearing round the corner and swept us both off our feet. I was only slightly bruised but my mother appeared to have hurt her leg badly. Lots of people helped her to the side of the road and an ambulance was called. We sat there in the sun, just talking, with my mother gasping every now and then with the pain. I said to her, 'It's just like you, isn't it, to get yourself run over.'

'Well,' she said, 'I can tell all my friends that I have been treated in an Italian hospital.'

There is one moment I will remember forever. As we sat there, a giant green lizard slowly came towards us, clambered over my knees and across and over my mother's knees. He stopped once to gaze at our faces and then wandered off somewhere into a bush. For some reason, I often think of that moment – it was magical. Very quickly the ambulance came – two spirited medics arrived and, muttering a lot of Italian, they lifted my mother onto the stretcher but were so busy looking at my breasts that, as they were trying to get the stretcher into the ambulance, they nearly tipped her off it. 'Excuse me, young man,' she shouted, 'would you mind taking your eyes off my daughter's cleavage.' They didn't understand and just laughed and so did we. Three days later, the hospital said my mother could go home – so home we went.

Chapter 11

NEW AWAKENING

Hair by Carl was now open and my mother was the receptionist. The salon was in Allerton, a suburb with mainly Jewish residents, and the ladies flocked to have their hair done. In those days, it was a time when male hairdressers were something new and much revered. Eric, now redundant, was the manager. It was a happy time: the three men in my life were occupied with something interesting; my mother had something to do with her friendly, smiling way and her sense of humour; Carl was going to get married to Annette, and Nigel was having a fiery relationship with Jackie.

They were both lovely girls, but suddenly Claremont was bulging at the sides with their highs and lows. Annette was a beautiful redhead with an endemic sense of drama. Normally, insignificant quarrels were tearful and resulted with Annette poised in the middle of a room, draped in her 'argumentative' clothes, which consisted of a lot of black, a hint of cleavage and hair arranged dramatically over her shoulders, with some kind of secret, bejewelled clip almost hidden in the sometimes black and sometimes deepest red hair. It was rather like watching a Shakespeare play, with Carl, pale and also in black, toing and froing from the room as a new and heartfelt speech was born in his mind.

Nigel and Jackie, however, were more down to earth. Jackie, also blonde and beautiful, would be enveloped in a white towel dressing gown, with bare feet and that 'just got up' natural blonde hair. Nigel was loud and accusing as she choked with pseudo tears. Her favourite speech was 'I hate your family, all stuck up they are, think they're someone, I hate all of them'.

Once, I happened to be passing as she delivered this outcry and she suddenly added, 'Except your mother'!

I quite enjoyed my family's rows. It gave me much to think about and more to write about. I had started writing desperate poetry and I also started writing a book called *Stopping Place*, a story about gypsies. The usual romantic stuff – they settle on some private land, the owner comes storming out, falls in love with the main character, Rhia, and so it went on to be potentially an interesting story, but the half I had written got lost during our movements from one house to another, so I stuck to my desperate poetry.

During this rather frustrating time, I received yet another call from the producer – more *Liver Birds* – when could I come down? And so it all started again, beginning with saying goodbye to Eric, who as usual wore his brave face, and boarding the train and waving to him until the train got near the bridge and then disappeared into the dark tunnel leading to the sunlit bridge, which always marked the real beginning of the journey. The difference was that Myra was not there to make me laugh. I drank coffee and ate a sandwich and looked again at all the back gardens, all of which I seemed to know so well, and the strange journey across London to a luxurious hotel which the BBC had now booked me into.

I stood in the lift as it journeyed several floors and walked along a corridor looking for room 109. I had hoped to feel better when I entered the room, but the green silk and dark wood and even the flowers screamed loneliness. I went to the window to look for comfort, but found only rather a grey area of Kensington High Street. There were several messages waiting for me – one from Eric, one from my sons and one from 'Him' who wanted to see me and talk things over, concerning the future of *The Liver Birds*.

He came to the hotel two hours after I arrived and we had coffee and sandwiches. It was a little awkward at first but something he said made me laugh and I could already feel that we were enjoying each other. The fact that I was married did not enter our conversation – we were supposed to be discussing *The Liver Birds* – but a great warmth had sprung up between us. I had never been a flirtatious person and only once had I been in other company where it was obvious the man in question was not looking for simple friendship and I had fled. But I did not want to flee from this man. And by the time he left, I felt as if I were being drawn into something which, on the one hand, made my heart turn over with worry, and on the other, turn over with excitement.

When I went back to my room there was another message – from Myra. It simply said: 'Go for it Ro' – which I felt was her way of distancing herself from our partnership. My head was a cobweb of worries. I decided to ring Eric and to retreat into what was my real world.

'Hello my darling, are you OK?'

'I'm fine.'

'Is the hotel nice?'

'It's brilliant.'

'Have you had your meeting yet?'

'No, tomorrow.'

'Well show them what you're made of sweetheart.'

'I will.'

'I love you.'

'I love you.'

Oh God, something was drifting towards me. It seemed to be filled with dread and guilt and all other words surrounding those two things.

The meeting was in the producer's office. Polly and Nerys were there, both looking gorgeous. They had so much easy conversation. I doubt if they had ever experienced shyness. They knew all the stars, all the important people in the BBC building. They were hugged and kissed by everybody in the corridors, and I found myself starting to describe Egor, my Wolfhound.

'He's huge,' I said, 'when he jumps to greet you his paws land on your chest.'

The two girls winced and the producer whispered, 'Bloody hell.'

Within minutes I was describing my cat, my parrot, the things my parrot said and suddenly I was seized with embarrassment. I did not know anybody important enough to boast about. Indeed, I was faced with three people who knew nothing about me or the kind of life I had lived, and I was gate crashing into their crazy, tinselled world talking about my dog, my cat and my parrot.

Suddenly, I started to talk about the character Sandra. 'I think she should be warm and terribly romantic,' I said. 'I think she should always defend the downtrodden and make excuses for them, and I think that Beryl could be more down to earth, seeing in people more of the things to beware of than to be praised.' I was on a non-stop ride now and it became more and more embarrassing. 'For instance,' I said, not knowing what the very next word was going to be, 'Sandra could bring home a puppy or a kitten. She would leap into the "Aahh" factor, whereas Beryl would say, "They smell".' I looked anxiously at Polly's face.

'I love dogs actually,' said Polly.

The producer saved me, 'But Carla is writing about Beryl,' he said softly.

Oh God, now I was in a typical script discussion.

And then, in unison with 'Him', she said, 'But this is Beryl, I know, I know.'

The conversation concerning dogs, however, went on for almost the whole meeting. I was sorry I ever mentioned them. And the producer was charming and open to all of it. We managed to laugh at many of the tales that we had to tell, and the meeting ended on a high note, but as I walked along the BBC corridor to the lift and stepped out into the main reception, I was dreading working with those two girls. It was not that they were not charming and it was not that they were not really nice people, but they seemed so powerful. The receptionist said, 'Shall I call you a taxi, Carla?'

A voice came, 'It's all right, I'll take her.' It was 'Him'.

We hardly spoke. It seemed that there were two different versions of us, us when we were at work and us when we were alone. Outside the hotel, we sat silently in his car.

'Will you be all right?' he said.

'Yes, yes, fine.'

'When are you going home?'

'When you let me.'

He smiled, 'I've got a few things I'd like to go over with you,' he said. 'I'll ring you from the office tomorrow, when I've looked at what Judy has got for me.' Judy being his devoted secretary.

'OK.'

I tried to get out of the car in a dignified fashion, but it never works. My bag got caught on the hand brake, the heel of my shoe got trapped in my long skirt. I landed on the pavement miraculously on my feet but it was hardly the work of a ballet dancer. He drove away smiling.

Chapter 12

HEARTACHE

So I was back in the television world again. Rehearsals had gone well. A couple of tiny differences broke out between Polly and me. She often questioned some of the dialogue and I had learned by now how to explain why I wrote the words in the script. Although they were always amicable, these quarrels sometimes became a little heated and I would find myself engaged in battle with two brilliant actresses who obviously knew more than I did about acting, questioning lines I had given them. As the days moved on, I became much more expert at handling these moments – giving a little, taking a little, trying to look as though I was cooperating, but basically I was always guarding the words that I had written.

The recording went smoothly, everybody was thrilled and I left the Television Centre with 'Him', in a satisfied mood. It was to be my usual lift home, but it was quite a long time before I realised that I did not recognise the route we were taking, and then I knew he was taking me to his flat.

'I thought you might like a cup of coffee,' he said.

It was probably the worst excuse I've ever heard but I didn't mind. I had known all along, since that first day we met, that something had to happen, but I was never sure what it would be. It was as if there was a plan and we were waiting for it to arrive. We drank coffee in his very bachelor-like flat and we listened to some classical music. I had not really acquainted myself with what seemed to me then to be the drone of Tchaikovsky, and with the other noises made by orchestra, tenors and sopranos, but those moments were the beginning of a great passion that I would have for classical music in the future.

I don't remember the journey to the bedroom. Indeed, nor did I register it at the actual time – we just seemed to arrive there. He was lying on the bed, hands behind his head, fully clothed, staring at the ceiling. I felt as if perhaps he wanted me to do a little dance or a comedy sketch for him – the word 'sex' didn't seem to apply to the situation. Soon, I too was lying on the bed beside him. I knew now where all this was going, and I began to worry about almost everything. Would he notice my rather untidy appendix scar? My breasts had always seemed reasonable but what would they look like when I was lying down? And how would I get my tights off without looking like a Sumo wrestler?

Accompanying these thoughts was the worry of whether this was right or was it wrong. I began to go through the probable consequences, but decided not to linger on them. Everything became slow and effortless. Soon, I was without my clothes, as well as my tights and we were, shock horror, in bed. There was nothing frantic – everything could have been set to slow, sweet music. There was no screaming and panting, nothing that would jeopardise our dignity – just a long gentle shiver, and the deed was done. We lay silently for a long time without speaking.

Outside my hotel, he called from his car, 'Are you all right?'

'Yes.'

'I'll call you tomorrow.'

'OK.'

'Bye.'

'Bye.'

I walked along the dark blue corridor of the hotel, passing my own room and doing a U-turn at the end. I was frozen with guilt. I pushed open the door and almost ran to phone Eric. He would have been ringing the hotel; what should I say? He'll know, he'll guess, oh God.

'Hello darling,' I said in a more than cheerily way.

'Hi, everything all right – did you have your meeting?'

'Yes, yes, it went well.'

'I forgot to tell you, darling, Leslie rang and asked me to go to the club. I would have phoned you but it was all in a hurry.'

'Well never mind, I'm phoning you.'

'Have you eaten yet?'

'Yes, I had a snack brought to my room and I watched television.'

'You must be lonely my darling.'

'No, well, yes, but it's all part of what I want to do. I have to pay up somewhere. Are the boys OK?'

'Yes, they're in their various parts of the house. There's a lot of music going on.'

'Is Egor all right?'

'He'd wet the carpet when I came in.' Then, to the dog: 'Who's a bad dog then, who's a really bad dog?'

'Ah,' I managed, 'he's young, he'll learn.'

The conversation continued for a long time. I lay in the bath trying to get my head together. I needed quiet, I needed to think things out. Had what happened really happened, or was I imagining it all. Finally, I moved to the edge of the bed, unable somehow to get into it, my head just wouldn't sort itself out. Where was I in life? It was a long, long time before I got to sleep. I dreaded tomorrow.

It so happened that 'tomorrow' was fine. We met a few more people we were going to cast – everyone was relaxed and laughing and afterwards 'He' ran me home. During the journey he said, 'I think it's time you bought yourself a car, you know.'

I thought, 'He's tired of running me home.' 'I will,' I said, 'I will. It's just that I don't know London and I don't like driving in places I'm not familiar with.' He put on his sexiest voice. 'You only have to know the way to Chiswick.'

Chapter 13

GOODBYE PADDINGTON

As I had moved from bed-sit to posh hotel, I felt it was time to have a place of my own in London. I found a flat in Paddington and fell in love with it immediately. While all the boring paperwork was being done, I made a brief visit home. Probably guilt drove me there. I needed to see Eric and how he was managing his wifeless existence and how my sons were coping with their overcrowded lives – all was well.

Not long afterwards, I sold my flat in Paddington in order to buy a beautiful house in Holland Park. It was at this time that my sister Marna and her husband Leonard decided that I needed looking after and asked if they could take on the task. I was elated. The house was a huge, five-storey, semi-detached Victorian building. At the back, it had a small courtyard and at the front a tiny sunken garden. I moved in with five cats, several birds of different kinds, a rabbit and a tortoise. On my last visit to Claremont, I had also brought back Egor, the family Irish wolfhound, who sat on the large sofa, begging with his eyes 'Please can I come with you?' He was ten years old now and it was lonely in the house with the family all so busy. 'Come on,' I said.

My relationship with 'Him' was growing ever stranger. We yo-yoed between his flat and my house. Neither of us knew what it was all about. It was as if fate was playing a game with us, clanging us together like a pair of cymbals and drowning out any intelligent thoughts on impact. We quarrelled most of the time, we cried and screeched at each other, left each other for some of the time and came back together for another round.

The Liver Birds was still going on and in truth was growing a little tired of it. A nice event that happened was when I received an award for the series. I cannot remember where the ceremony was held but it was in some posh place in London. There were five hundred people present and Sir Lew Grade made the presentation.

To keep our secret, I asked a very dear friend, Norman Crisp, a great writer of television drama to accompany me. Almost from the first day of entering the BBC he had become a friend. He had a flat in Paddington close to mine and he remained there after I moved to Holland Park. It was a very grand affair – the room was filled with glittering people who all seemed immensely beautiful. The ladies were wearing gowns that I would never have tried to compete with. I sat at the table with Sir Lou Grade and his friends, and throughout it all I could not quite believe why I was there. This was my first public encounter and I could feel myself trembling the whole time. I managed to climb the red-carpeted steps onto the stage. I have no idea what I said to the audience, apart from the word 'thank you'.

Sir Lew handed me the award, which was in a red-and-gold box. I held it up for the audience to see and started to leave the stage. The trophy then fell through the bottom of the box, which was all I needed to complete my terror. I gathered it up and fled from the stage to the sound of clapping. As I got half way back to my table and began to feel the comfort of having escaped, I became aware that Sir Lou was following me and waving something. The faster he went, the faster I went and he did not catch up with me until I reached my table and the comforting arms of my friend Norman. Sir Lou held up an envelope and said, 'I have five hundred pounds here for Carla but she doesn't seem to want it.' Everybody clapped but to me it was just another nail in my lack of confidence coffin.

On the way home Norman said, 'Don't worry about it. Just think: five hundred people will be talking to their friends about you for days. What more do you want woman?' Sadly, Norman became ill and had to go home to Southampton where he died just months later. I will always think of him as my mentor. He was a brilliant writer but he never boasted about his achievements, though he was always boasting about mine. We often sat in a little French restaurant in Paddington and he changed my views on life completely. He was the only person who knew about my relationship with 'Him' and was clever enough not actually to mention it but to remind me what a talented producer he was. I always took that to mean that he approved of the relationship. He was a brilliant man without vanity.

The Liver Birds was now coming to an end, but I was accustomed to my new life. The BBC held no fear for me any more. As I walked through the various corridors it was 'Hi Carla', 'Hello gorgeous', 'You've done it again I see', etcetera. I had managed to shake off the feelings of inferiority with which I had arrived in London. At one time, it was difficult for me to be in the bar surrounded by hugely talented people, most of them doing so much more important work than The Liver Birds, but strangely this series seemed to endear people to me and even the most famous offered their congratulations. It is not hard to be among show business people; it seems that the higher they rise, the more polite, the more generous they are. They are eager with their praise and, contrary to the picture painted, I found nothing but loyalty.

It was at about this time that I met Michael Winner, who lived in a beautiful, enormous house close to mine. He rang me and said, 'I have a proposition for you – let's have lunch.' We sat at the end of a long, carved table and were served by a small, softly spoken, Scottish lady. She was obviously a loyal friend and servant of his. The meal itself and everything connected to the ritual of it was flawless. Michael's proposition was that I joined his company and write for them. Obviously, I thought a lot about this, but in my heart I knew it wouldn't be the kind of writing I wanted to do.

The next day, I found myself in the company of the Head of Comedy and innocently I told him about this offer. He seemed rather neutral about it and we went straight into a discussion about another idea that I was turning over in my mind called *Butterflies*. I had only been home less than an hour when I had a phone call from the Head of Comedy at the BBC. He said that he had thought about my invitation from Michael and suggested that I should now go on contract with the BBC. At first, I didn't realise the importance of this, but when I told 'Him', he said it was the first time he'd heard of such a thing and he hugged me and said, 'Well done darling, well done.' Michael didn't make things difficult for me when finally I refused his offer and told him about the BBC's contract. 'Go where you are happy, girl, go where you are happy.'

'Are you angry,' I asked.

'Why should I be angry,' he replied. 'Do it my dear, do it, and good luck to you.'

He disappeared into a large cupboard and brought out an original drawing in a gold frame and handed it to me. 'Have this,' he said. People can be very snide about Michael, but I found him to be a fair-minded man and once a friend always a friend, provided you don't annoy him, and the picture hangs proudly in my house to this day.

Chapter 14

VISITED BY BUTTERFLIES

And so the story of *The Liver Birds* closed. In spite of the fact that I had written over eighty scripts, I still felt like a newcomer. Nerys and Polly made it easy for me. They had both loved it but it was getting hard to play very young girls now and neither one of them wanted to be referred to as the Liver Birds for the rest of their career. The last show was a very emotional time for all of us, but now I was free from the rigours of rehearsals, sets and costumes. I felt that perhaps I would never have such a great time in any future show that I managed to write, and my old familiar friend, fear, returned as I walked out of the studio that night. We had had a good long run of praise and publicity and now I was haunted by *Butterflies*.

The idea came to me when I was thinking about my own life. What a mess it seemed to be. Now distanced from Eric, but still his wife, I was seized with guilt and self-hate for how selfish I had been. Although there was only one incident with 'Him', I knew that there was something very special growing between us. There were endless little liaisons: a drive into the countryside, then to a little café which no one else in the whole world seemed to know about; walks in distant woodlands with Egor bounding between us, or sitting in either his flat or my house listening to music. It was not all about sex – sex seemed to be the distant goal somehow. I realise how old-fashioned we were compared to the way things are now, but old-fashioned or not it was still dangerous for a married person to have an affair. He was not like Eric in any way. I found myself wondering why I had chosen to care for only two men in my life and both were cloaked in secrecy – secrecy of thoughts, secrecy of feelings. Neither wanted to be seen actually to need me – Eric came near to this sometimes, but only in anger, and he obviously felt that to want my company was the greatest gift he could give me but I have to guess the rest. To most people this would be unacceptable and even as I write about it I can hear you saying 'What! What!' but my reward was intrigue.

I went to see John Howard Davies, who was now the new Head of Comedy. He was young, attractive and a risk taker, but when I told him that I wanted to write about a woman who was married but falling in love with another man he shook his head decidedly. 'No, no, darling,' he said, 'not in comedy. Drama perhaps – write me a play instead.'

'But John, she doesn't actually have an affair. She meets him in the park and no doubt he occupies her fantasies, and compared with her very proper but very charming husband, he spells excitement.'

John shook his head, 'Not in comedy darling, we'll get the entire viewing public against us.'

I was becoming frustrated.

'But why – she doesn't go to bed with him.' I almost said, 'Except once,' but I curbed myself as I began to get mixed up with *Butterflies* the series and my personal Butterflies that was us.

I raised my voice, 'I don't understand, I don't understand – I'm talking about life.'

He lowered his voice and was very gentle now, 'But she wants to go to bed with him, doesn't she?'

'Yes, but . . .'

'That is the problem darling, her intent – it's for drama not comedy.'

All my pleading failed and I stormed out of the BBC feeling as if someone had tied chains around my mind.

When I got home, there were two messages, one from Eric and one from 'Him'. Eric's said, 'Will you be home for your birthday? Would you like to go to the theatre?' I didn't listen to the second message. I picked up my pen and began to write. I could not stop, words flowed, nothing put me off, I hadn't even made plans for this first script and yet, two days later, there it was – completed. I put it in an envelope and despatched it to John Howard Davies' office. The very next day, a message was sent to me by motorbike. It read, 'Who am I to argue with a Butterfly – six more please. Love John.'

To add to the chaos, I had now decided to move yet again – to Zoffany House which was on the river bank in Chiswick. I had sold my Holland Park house to Ruby Wax.

When she came to view it, she made me laugh. She was accompanied by a man whom she described as 'my lawyer'. It is difficult to explain just how funny Ruby is. She has this humour lurking behind almost every sentence. For instance, during the time she was looking through the house, the estate agent had also sent two Chinese people to look at it. While Ruby was sitting on the settee talking to her lawyer, these two quiet, nervous people walked through the room. Ruby's remark to me was, 'So who arranged for the Far East to come here?' She then asked if she could please phone the agent, which she did. Her side of the conversation went as follows: 'So we have Chinatown here.' Pause. 'But I am buying this house.' Pause. 'Yes, buying, with money. OK, OK. I'm coming to the office. I will begin by throwing your typewriter out of the window, followed by you. Thank you.' She put the phone down. Then Ruby presented me with a lovely wide smile and said, 'OK, I think I can live here.'

After she had moved into the house, she invited me round to collect my mail and have a cup of coffee. She was preparing her husband's meal. The table was set and she placed a tin of tuna on the dinner mat, a lettuce leaf in a bowl and a knife and fork. When he came in he said, 'I'm sorry honey, I haven't time to eat, I've got to get back to the office.' And Ruby said, quite seriously, 'After I've gone to all this trouble?' The next time I met her, our cars pulled up side by side. She was heavily pregnant. 'Hi, Ruby,' I said, 'how are you?' Ruby replied, 'Hi Carla. It just won't come out. It must be at least a year old,' and off she drove.

Zoffany House was a listed building and had been the home of the eighteenth-century painter Johann Zoffany. It had everything that I had ever dreamed of. At the back, there was a large, paved garden and next door grew a splendid old oak tree which seemed to have chosen my garden in which to spread most of its branches. Running the full length of this garden was a room that consisted primarily of beautiful old windows – not a conservatory but more like a glass studio –which soon became an aviary, and a tiny lily pond that would soon become an enormous fishpond. There was a reasonably ordinary kitchen, though it had an old sink and an old, tiled floor. From there, one entered what I was to call the Marble Hall. A huge arch led into the hall and it stretched right along to the front door. I was so excited by it, but the best was yet to come. As you opened the front door, there was the river. The house was separated from it by a small, railed garden. I envisaged my dogs and cats sitting in this little paradise, safe from other dogs, other cats and traffic. Marna and Len took the four rooms at the top of the house. This, I felt, was a brave decision, as they had already shared the total chaos of my life and were now ready to do it all again.

It didn't take me long to settle in. I was able to write *Butterflies* out in my tiny front garden with the River Thames flowing by, little red sailing yachts passing by and ducks and geese swimming along – all pleasant and gentle things. Although there was more drama that was to follow, it was one of the happiest times of my life.

One day, when I was driving along the Portobello Road, I noticed some kids kicking something around between them. To my horror, I saw it was a baby pigeon. I braked hard, jumped out of my car and, in spite of much beeping and shouting, I ran to pick him up. The driver of the bus behind shouted, 'Go on, you silly bitch.' I went to him and said politely, 'And you are an ignorant bastard.'

It took me some minutes to find a comfortable way to carry this little bird, which was soaked in blood and gasping. I wrapped him in some newspaper that was on the seat of my car and put him carefully on my knee. During the journey, I decided to call him Bell, and when I got home I fed him tiny crumbs and put him in a small cage. I thought it best to leave his wounds until the next day so as not to frighten him, but in truth I felt certain that he would be dead. But no, there he was, bright eyed, no longer gaping, ready for breakfast. I fed him, then carefully washed all the blood away and put some antiseptic powder on the wound. Then I put him in the studio safely away from my cats. Less than a week later, while I was dressing his wound, Bell managed to fly down to the floor before I could retrieve him, but clearly my cats quite liked him and he quite liked them, and for ever more he wandered among them freely, pinched their food, drank from their water dish and became a proper member of our family. Although my cats lived to a ripe old age, they are now gone, but guess what, Bell is still here and seventeen years old.

The tranquillity of Zoffany House was shattered two years later. I was still travelling to Liverpool, still married to Eric but the problem was that I could no longer live this dual existence. In order to survive emotionally, I decided that I had to ask Eric for a divorce. He met me as usual at Lime Street Station. Without doubt he was noticeably unhappy, if not charged with anger. He seemed not even to suspect me of seeing anyone else, but today, when I think about it, I'm sure that he did. I tried to explain to him as best I could that I wanted to leave him. My speech was very dramatic: 'I have grown away from you – away from our life together. It has nothing to do with television, it would have happened anyway, just differently that's all. I will always love that you are the father of our sons, that you worked very hard to build a life for us, but it must go now. I need freedom and when you get over this anger you will realise that you, too, need freedom and you will have time to build another life.'

We made an attempt to hug each other but we were rigid and he was pale and angry. I walked away half relieved, half insane with sorrow. I had witnessed in the past how really angry he could become and a sense of fear overtook me. As I walked through the hall, I looked up and saw Eric's face. He was looking down over the upstairs banisters – it was a picture of the sheerest sorrow. We stared at each other for a moment – my legs were trembling and could hardly carry me to my taxi. I had to get away now.

The train journey back to London was filled with a sense of not being sure of anything. I decided not to tell Carl or Nigel or my mother just yet what had happened. I also warned myself now that whether or not my other relationship existed my marriage certainly did not. I replayed the seriousness of what happened in Liverpool and mentioned casually to 'Him' that I was going to leave Eric, but that it was separate from him and me and it was not meant to affect us in any way. He smiled that long remembered smile and ruffled my hair. 'Jesus,' I thought, 'why do I only seem to attract men who swap conversation for a ruffle of the hair?'

Chapter **15**

HAPPINESS

Gareth Gwenlan was the producer chosen for *Butterflies*. When he told me that they had chosen Geoffrey Palmer to play Ben, I was thrilled, but when he told me that they had chosen Wendy Craig to play Ria, I was opposed. 'No, no, no,' I said, bearing in mind another series in which she had played a forever-whining mother of three. Gareth suggested that I meet her at least and we met in her office. I was filled with worry as to how I was going to make it clear to all concerned that Wendy in my mind was not right. The Head of Comedy was present as well as several other people concerned with the casting of the show. I was feeling very uneasy and wanted to get the whole thing over. I heard her voice in the corridor and when she came through the door to greet me I thought she looked fantastic. As she hugged me she said quietly, 'Carla, thank you for rescuing me from a morass of ordinariness. Your script is beautiful.' I must admit this threw me completely but, still feeling anxious, I sat in what turned out to be wonder as she and Geoffrey Palmer together with Nicholas Lyndhurst and Andrew Hall, who played the two sons, read the script. It all came out with complete sincerity. Wendy knew that she must make it clear that she loved Ben and no matter how many scenes she would journey through in the company of Leonard she knew that she must save it from turning into

68

just another boring, affair-type series. I was bowled over by her.

We filmed in Cheltenham. It was during late spring and early summer. For me, it was like seeing my own life unfolding. Wendy and Bruce Montague, who played Leonard, gave all the gentle subtlety needed and Geoffrey, as always, got every line, every wince, every half smile, right. His face, which was built with disapproval, and that wonderful, non-committal voice, the gentleness of Wendy and the charm of Bruce all made me feel completely contented with the possibilities of this series. When I wrote these scripts, I really believed that it all came from my own mind, but watching it being performed I realised that the whole thing was motivated by my own experiences.

I truly enjoyed every moment of *Butterflies*. Watching these exceptional people saying all the words in exactly the way I had heard them in my head as I wrote them was an amazing experience. I was still basically new in television – this was only my second series. I was certainly not an old hand at writing, and yet there I was gliding along as if it had been part of my whole life. However, there were hiccups. Halfway through the series another producer was assigned to *Butterflies* as Gareth was busy with something else. The other producer was 'Him', so there we were again stuck together in a situation which made it difficult for us to keep the secrecy of our relationship.

All went well for a while and then, one day, when we were filming in Cheltenham, a little knock came on my hotel room door. A voice said, 'Is it OK for me to come in?'

It was 'Him'.

I refrained from grasping his lapels and towing him in.

'I'm sorry,' he said, 'this is not the best situation for us, well for you anyway.'

'It's OK,' I said. 'It's fine, it's work.'

'Are you OK?'

'Yes, yes.'

'Do you approve of what I'm doing?'

'Yes, the filming's beautiful. I love that little lake where Ria and Leonard walk together.'

He then launched into a long explanation of how he envisaged the scene, how this would be, how that would be and as I watched him I felt a great tide of excitement. He suddenly stopped talking. 'I'm boring the arse off you,' he said.

'Yes,' I said.

We locked the bedroom door.

Later that week, as I was watching a scene being played in a small woodland, I didn't recognise the dialogue. The scene was between Ben and one of his sons. I whispered to Wendy, 'There's something wrong, isn't there?'

'Darling,' she said, 'it's not quite the dialogue you wrote.'

I remembered the words they were supposed to say and fearfully I stepped forwards and confronted 'Him'. 'That is not the line I wrote,' I said.

'I know,' he said, 'I've discussed it with them. Don't you think it's better?'

'No,' I said, 'no I don't.'

He sighed and walked back to the actors and carried on. I don't know why but a great fury flared up inside me. Not so much because the line had been changed, although that was bad enough, but because I hadn't been told or even consulted. They went through the scene again using the different dialogue. Real rage gripped me. Looking back I realised that what happened during that scene had little to do with the cause of my rage, it was the fact that we had to be so polite to each other, so distant – the fact that we had been so close a few hours before, and now suddenly he had become a stranger and I seemed to have ceased to exist. Wendy whispered to me, 'Don't worry Carla darling, we'll talk to him later.'

'I'll see you,' I said. 'Thank you Wendy.' And I walked blindly away, jumped into my car and drove back to London.

The next day, I raced to Liverpool. I wanted things to look really bad – I wanted my anger to be noticed, and not once during the journey did I relent. I kept repeating this tiny event over and over in my mind and as I did it grew bigger and bigger – he'd let me down, he hadn't talked to me first, I hated him. Before I left I had confided in Marna about all the pandemonium and as I packed my bag I quoted everything to her. As usual, she treated me to another sample of her unchangeable sense of humour. In an exaggeratedly posh voice she said, 'Go where you will, my dear. The more you disappear the more reason the neighbours will have to think that this bloody great house is mine.'

As I was packing, I spotted the day's post on my bed. I sat down to read it – the usual stuff – 'Could you send my daughter a photograph?' 'Could you tell me how to write for television?' – a mass of little cards fell from another envelope – 'Could you please sign each one of these? One for my grandfather, one for Helen,' one for this person, one for that – a couple of bills and somebody who wanted me to rescue a horse – and so it went on. Then I saw another envelope – it was different – rather important looking. I opened it and read it, not once, not twice, but several times. I was to be awarded the OBE. 'Oh, my God, it's a joke,' I thought. It went on: 'for my artistic contribution towards television.' I was just about to rush out and notify the entire world when I noticed that it was to be held in total confidence until after the announcement. I sat on the edge of the bed and read it again. Finally, I believed it.

Although by now I had bought myself a car, I was still a bit fearful of driving to Liverpool and back, so for Egor and me, it was yet another train journey. This time 'He' was not there to see me off, and Eric would not be there to greet me. I decided that being rich and famous was not as exciting as it seems. While I was playing out my own everlasting dramas, my sons were playing out theirs, but Eric seemed to be having a little liaison with the lady who used to massage him. I moved into my mother's part of Claremont. Eric and I occasionally passed each other silently in the main hall. It was summer time. I played with Egor on the great lawn, my mother sitting on the raised, grass slope, reading her book. She looked more like my sister than my mother. I loved being with her. She had a mean sense of humour and when she had delivered a remark, she would laugh helplessly holding her hand in front of her mouth and rocking. We had many strange little conversations. I remember one in particular. I happened to say to her, 'It was Daddy who taught me to care about animals, you know.'

She replied, 'No, it was me.'

'No Mummy,' I said, 'it was Daddy.'

'Rubbish,' she said, 'I was the one.'

Bearing in mind how my mother always liked to be dressed immaculately, I said, 'OK, here's the scenario: you are walking along the road. It is cold and windy and wet. You see on the other side of the road a pigeon. He's sick and he's stuck in the mud. What would you do? Would you call a neighbour to rescue him? Would you stop a car and ask them to rescue him? Or would you go and rescue him yourself?'

She fixed her dark brown eyes on me and said, 'Well, it depends what shoes I had on.'

I was still angry with 'Him'. I had not been in touch with him nor he with me. I felt rather silly having had romantic thoughts about 'Him' and me and us and love. One evening, I turned out the lights in Zoffany House, and sat in the dark watching the river. Egor was asleep downstairs in the kitchen. A great cloud of loneliness descended on me. I yearned for days of ordinariness – just walking my dog, playing with my children, laughing with my mother – but it all seemed so far away so – gone. I suddenly saw a movement by my gate – he stood looking up at the house – it was 'Him'. The initial excitement was quelled by the fact that I had no makeup on, my hair was wet from my bath, I was wearing a well loved but tatty dressing gown and as our relationship was still juvenile, I dashed upstairs and put on my black velvety one, after which I feverishly ransacked my makeup drawer grabbing any kind of facial camouflage, brushed my hair to make it look tousled and sexy and calmly went down the stairs wearing my best smile. My vision was that he would stand there, sort of embarrassed by his desperate need to see me, and we would end up in a passionate huddle on the doorstep. The only problem was – he'd gone.

As usual, sadness was lurking. Egor developed kidney trouble that quickly turned to kidney failure and I had to have him put to sleep. More tears, more rushing about trying to conduct my life, and still more tears when I was alone, just thinking of that beautiful, black-slightly-turning-grey face and those eyes – those eyes. We buried him in Claremont's garden. Needless to say, within two weeks, I had found another wolfhound, and guess what, I named him Egor.

After this it was back to Cheltenham to attend the filming. It would have been inappropriate for me to do otherwise. The scene was one in which Ria and Leonard sat on a bench by the familiar little pond. They were surrounded by green and growing things, three passing ducks intruded into the film and the weeping willow draped its branches in all the right places so that they seemed framed by its green curtain. He and I hardly spoke. I think both of us had decided that our struggling affair was best put on hold until our work was finished. Neither of us mentioned his visit the previous night.

During this time I had become friends with Rita Tushingham, a fine actress and wonderful company. Rita had a wicked sense of humour. Often, when we were having lunch in some posh restaurant, she would bring out from her handbag a strange collection of little toys, all of which wound up and toddled around the table. There were thumping rabbits, racing cars and little people in various guises. Rita herself, apart from winding them up, seemed not to notice them after that. It was as if they were her family, and something even more bizarre – I would look away for a moment to laugh behind my hand and when I looked back – she would be wearing a huge black moustache and a pair of National Health-style glasses. It was a strange, but likeable trait. Even the waiters got to know them so well that they passed no comment, and her facial disguises grew more and more bizarre as time went on. Like me, she was in the ebb and flow of a divorce. She invited me to Cornwall to stay with her in her beautiful house on the rocks. The idea was that I was supposed to keep her company during this stressful time, but it also did me a service. My mother always quoted her favourite cliché: 'Absence makes the heart grow fonder.' And as I clambered perilously amongst slippery rocks, jagged stones and raging seas that surrounded Rita's house, my mother's quote seemed appropriate.

Butterflies was now nearing the end of filming. Of course, we had the usual party and the obligatory exchanging of gifts, the hugging and kissing and murmuring sentences like 'You were wonderful', 'Darling, you were wonderful'. The boys had been well pleased with their parts and had served me well. It was all very emotional. We exchanged telephone numbers and addresses, we made speeches about each other, and there was more hugging, more kissing, more 'Darling, you were brilliant', more of all the ingredients of the end of every show. I was sorry to see *Butterflies* finished – I really did believe that I would never be able to write anything as good as that again.

Chapter **16**

LIFE WITH BREAD

It was a sad time when *Butterflies* ended. I had grown so fond of the cast, but one always has to move on – everything has its time. I will always treasure the friendship I had with the cast, but now my mind had begun putting out tentacles about the next idea. It happened in Kensington. I was parked in the High Street, thinking, thinking, 'What can I write about next?' I went through various panic stages, quite convinced that there was nothing left for me to say, but then, on the opposite side of the road, a young man walked – slowly, proudly. He was tall, straight, fair and was surrounded somehow with dignity. He was dressed all in black and I glimpsed a gold watch on his wrist – in fact, he was beautiful and as I watched him until I could turn my head no further, *Bread* was born.

The series would begin with Joey, my Kensington High Street stranger. My immediate thought was that Joey, in order to stand out, would have to come from a tough Liverpool family, but have charisma and a large helping of dignity. He, too, would be dressed in black and have a gold wristwatch. Having got him together, I didn't quite know what to do with him, so I decided to give him a mother, Mrs Boswell, played eventually by Jean Boht. Then, I gave her a daughter, Aveline. I decided to give Mrs Boswell four sons and a daughter in total. Of course, it seemed necessary now that she should have a husband, and that the family should have a grandfather, and as it grew in my head, the father should have an affair and suddenly I saw Mrs Boswell as the terrifying matriarch who loved her family, ruled her family and who needed at all times to be proud of her family. It was all so easy. I just sat in that car and by the time I drove home I had got it all sorted; they were alive and well in my head and I couldn't wait to pick up my pen.

The BBC accepted the idea of *Bread*, not with great passion but they had been so used to me haunting the offices with my ideas that they found it easier just to say, 'Yes, go ahead for God's sake'.

Before I could begin these scripts, I decided to go back to Liverpool and do some research. I needed to know the workings of Social Security and all the government departments dealing with people and their financial dilemmas, all of which would be relevant to my newly formed Boswell family. The man I spoke to in the Social Security office was incredibly dry and typically Northern. He began to tell me about the various things which had happened recently. Apparently, they had made a decision to give some extra money to any families which contained someone who was incontinent. The way they planned to do it was to give them £30 a week towards hiring or buying a washing machine. In his own words, with the Liverpool accent which I love so much, he said, 'Well, within twenty-four hours, the whole bloody city became incontinent. You couldn't tell the genuine ones from the rest. It wasn't just Grandma and Auntie May. Oh no, young lads and girls, some of them actually had doctor's notes disclosing their inability to hold their water.'

I was enjoying these encounters. 'Anyway,' he concluded, 'we scrapped that and we came up with another brilliant idea. Because there was quite a lot of violence in the city and robbery and things, we decided we would help them towards buying a guard dog. Five minutes after the announcement, every bugger in Liverpool owned a dog, and they all started claiming for its food, its lead, its collar. So we sent men round to check on these people and their newly found guard dogs. Every one of them answered the front door with either a bloody miniature type dog with a pink bow round its neck or a vicious, bloody upstart with teeth like a fucking crocodile.'

All this made *Bread* important to me and exciting, although I didn't use the actual stories.

The rehearsal of *Bread* was full of fun, anticipation, comradeship. The cast enjoyed the scripts and I enjoyed how they portrayed it in the read through. Now they were coming to Liverpool to film. Robin Nash, the chosen producer of *Bread* was a tall, hunk of a man, in his late fifties. He was admittedly and unashamedly gay; his partner's name was Andreas. They were dignified men and did not, like some, display their gayness. He always wore a little bow tie and sometimes a bright yellow scarf. We all loved him and I could see that *Bread* was going to be a lovely adventure. Christine Mellor, from now on called Chrissie, typed all my scripts for me and sorted out any changes made to them. She was the production assistant and, I have to say, she enjoyed the company and the attention of all the young men in the cast.

From the very beginning, we laughed throughout the rehearsals. Peter Howitt played the part of Joey, the young man I saw in Kensington High Street, with great dignity and, of course, the female viewers went wild about him. In fact, all the cast, so carefully chosen by Robin, played their parts perfectly. Anyone who watched *Bread* all those years ago will remember Jean Boht as Mrs Boswell. Jean was someone who had come up through the acting world searching for 'This is it, this is what I've been looking for', and she found this in *Bread*. One day, Jean came into rehearsal late. 'I've been rescuing a baby duck,' she said. 'I found it walking by my house. I kept taking it back to the pond, putting it there and it kept sinking, so I had to bring it in with me.' She turned to me, 'Will you go and look at it Carla, there must be something wrong with it, it couldn't swim.' I went immediately. 'This little duck must be injured,' I thought. 'This little duck is malformed or sick.' I opened Jean's car door and there, sitting in a box on the front seat, was a baby pigeon!

What an inspiration Jean was. Because the cast were all young and some playing an important part for the first time, she was always there, guiding and teaching them and would never let them off with the slightest slip. And if they did not turn up one morning perhaps, for rehearsal, she would almost pin them against the wall and say, 'I have waited all my acting life for a part like this. They don't come often and mostly not at all, and *you* stroll in here a day late for rehearsal, giving excuses like 'my car wouldn't start'.' She would then screech, 'Then get a bloody taxi, you're being paid enough.' If the excuse was 'I had a headache', the answer would be: 'So take a bloody aspirin.'

I knew by the nature of these outbursts that she loved each and every one of them and that the affection was returned, and without realising it she was simply, in real life, being Mrs Boswell. Her generosity was mega. At the end of each series, everybody would receive a present, and often she had gone to the trouble, if the present was silver or such like, of having names engraved. She said to me at the end of the series, 'I have never been as happy as I have been in *Bread*.'

It was during these rehearsals that the day of my investiture of the OBE came. I remember getting up in the morning and finding it difficult to believe. My sons were hurtling down from Liverpool and I wondered if I could possibly keep calm when my head was full of all my problems: 'Him' and me, the fact that I had filed for a divorce and that Eric was behaving rather irrationally at home. However, by the time my sons arrived, some kind of order came. My sons had explained to my mother what was happening and she was cemented in her chair, imagining that it was going to be on the television. Before I could explain, she said, 'You won't wear those awful shoes will you, flat things with a black buckle. I don't know why, but I always think of Napoleon when I see them. And you won't go the opposite way and wear very high heels will you. You know how you wobble in them . . .'

'No, no, mother, I won't be wearing flat shoes or high rise shoes, something in the middle, OK?'

'Don't let the Queen frighten you,' she said, 'we all go to the lavatory.'

She was not just my mother; she was all the things a human being should be.

Carl drove us to the Palace. My beloved old Mercedes bore proudly a noticeable green pass that had been placed in the front window. There was a huge crowd outside, and when we reached the courtyard we were engulfed by the press. My sons were directed to one entrance at the Palace and I to another. There was a long, richly decorated hall, which seemed to stretch before me for miles. Every few yards, sentries stood to rigor mortis-type attention, their faces carved out of stone, not a tremble of the lips nor a flicker of the eye. On each side, the walls were hung with large, important paintings and, with great joy, I spotted one by Zoffany. It was difficult for me not to say to one of the guards 'I live in his house', but instead I stood staring at it. To think that a man so talented had actually lived, slept and laboured in what was now my home. I tried to imagine just where he died – was it upstairs or downstairs, in the garden, in bed, was it my bedroom or Marna and Len's bedroom? A few people began to overtake me, so I followed them to the end of the passage, which led to an enormous, richly decorated room. There, a man in full regalia greeted all of us and began to show us exactly what we were supposed to do when receiving our medals.

One by one, we were called and when my name was heard I was guided to a smaller room, which led into a large room where a huge audience waited. Somewhere an orchestra was playing. I stood waiting for the person before me to receive their OBE so that I could go forwards. The sweet and innocent music calmed me a little, but when one of the ushers waved me on, I suddenly seemed to lose consciousness – I don't even remember walking to the Queen. I was madly going over, 'Three steps forwards, two steps back, a bow, a quick turn and off through that draped door at the other side. OK, I've got it, OK, I've got it.'

The Queen seemed quite small. She was wearing a yellow silk suit, or it could have been linen. I remember it looked slightly creased and I was surprised by that. I went to hold out my hand but I remember the man wearing the full regalia saying something about 'do not touch Her Majesty', so I quickly withdrew it. She smiled her brilliant smile. 'I believe you write for television,' she said.

'Yes, Your Majesty,' I said.

'Well done,' she said.

'Thank you, Your Majesty,' I said.

I think she then said 'You have come a long way forward in the media.'

'Thank you, Your Majesty,' I said.

Now what? 'Three steps back, turn to the right, get away as quickly as you know how.'

The orchestra suddenly played a rather more lively tune, which seemed to say, 'Get off, get off,' so off I went, through the door opposite with a sign of absolute relief. Suddenly, I realised that I did not recognise where I was. It was a narrow passage that curved round. I passed some windows and it led to an opening that didn't seem to be where I was supposed to be. However, I went through a door, and to my horror I was back on the stage where I had begun. The gentleman who normally greeted OBE recipients could not believe what he was seeing, as, in sheer terror, I walked once again across the stage, past the Queen and towards what I knew now was the original, proper door. There was a gentle outbreak of laughter among the audience and the orchestra played a tune which had the same tempo as 'Here we go again'. As soon as I got to the right place I sat on a cushioned window seat and died one of those deaths.

Outside, in the Palace courtyard, photographers were taking pictures, each one placing their subjects in the same pose – husbands and sons holding their top hats and draping their grey silk gloves over their arm. Although I did not enjoy the pose I was placed in, I behaved and held back the giggle that was stuck in my throat at the sight of all of us standing there clutching our little black boxes.

The next morning the papers were full of it. The headlines read: 'Carla gets the gong,' 'Top scriptwriter goes to Palace.' I was wearing my favourite long, black silk skirt and my three-quarter-length black velvet coat, graced with long Victorian beads and comfortable shoes. I looked like everybody's grandmother. When I got back to the house, there was a telephone message from 'Him'. He picked me up and we went to a small hotel buried in a little Welsh village. We walked by little streams, climbed manageable little hills and lay in the dark on a little bed of dandelions – our passionate contribution to the conservation of wild flowers.

*

One day, the singer Chrissie Hynde invited me to her flat to meet some friends. It was also to be a gathering to discuss the welfare of animals, a subject that I had almost abandoned, but in which now my interest was alive again. There were a few well known pop singers there – I can't remember who – but they were enthusiastic and Chrissie, a strong minded, hugely attractive lady, knelt in the centre of the room and gave her passionate reasons why we should all care and fight for other creatures. As she was speaking, a blonde lady suddenly said, 'You are talking about animals and their plight, but I see you are wearing a leather skirt.'

We have all been caught with that one in our beginnings, but Chrissie was calm. 'Yes,' she replied, 'and who knows, if I can get this meeting in order and discuss what we are here to discuss, I might never wear one again.'

I loved them both right away. When I bravely ventured that we should all pull together and form a noticeable group of protestors against cruelty, the blonde lady applauded me louder than the rest. Before the meeting ended she came to me and handed me a little note. It had her telephone number and her signature, which I didn't study at that time. I came across it sometime later but could not read the surname. However, I rang her, and we went straight into the animal situation, namely that for twenty years we had cared and worried about animals and suddenly she said, 'Come on down and see us – let's get something together, Paul will be here.' I realised for the first time that I was speaking to Linda McCartney. I didn't make any little noises when this thought occurred to me and I said goodbye to her and then sat, whispering to myself, 'Oh my God, oh my God, I've been talking to Linda McCartney.'

A few days later, I found myself at her home in Rye, sitting in front of her piano, with her bashing out a tune and me bashing out words to go with it. Now and then, Paul would put his head round the door, raise his eyes to heaven and walk out again. Eventually, I asked Paul if he would play a part for me in *Bread*. 'Just a small part,' I said. He replied, 'You write it, I'll read it and I might do it, our Carla.'

In this episode Linda and Mrs Boswell were having a cup of tea together and Mrs Boswell asked Linda, 'Has your chap got a job?' Linda replied, 'Yes, sort of.' This, of course, delighted the viewers and more so when Paul arrived in his big car outside the Boswell house at the same time as Joey was parking his car. We faded down on his face when he saw whom his mother was chatting to. After that climax, Linda and I went on trying to write songs. Although we had the passion, neither of us had the equipment, that is, to play the piano really well and to sing in tune. Consequently, we always ended up with many fine words and that was all. So we went to the kitchen and tried to bring about a plan that would stop the entire world eating animals. It was even harder than writing songs, but I treasure those times I had with Linda.

Chapter **17**

THE BEST OF DAYS

It was a Sunday. I was happy. I had tossed out all the agitation, aggravations and misunderstandings into the air and they had blown away leaving a clear blue happy sky. 'He' and I were going out for the day. We hadn't decided where, we were going to let the car just take us and see where we ended up. I was excited because we were both in a good frame of mind. We had stopped trying to analyse our relationship. I had finished writing another series of *Bread* and was waiting for rehearsals to begin. All was well.

The news came on the radio and I turned it up so that I could listen to it in the bathroom as I got ready. I heard the word Liverpool on the radio news. Whenever I hear that word I want to hear more so I trotted back into the lounge. The newscaster was saying that there had been an accident on the River Mersey, a boat had collided with a ferry. I was sorry, of course; it must have been awful, but then my heart leapt when he said the *Lady Irene* – that was my son Carl's boat – oh my God! I was seized with instant panic. Instead of getting ready to go out with 'Him', I started quickly getting ready to go to Liverpool. In between trying to ring various parts of Claremont House where my whole family lived, I rushed about, packing a small case, trying to be calm, telling myself that it need not be Carl's boat, perhaps there was another *Lady Irene*. I called a taxi and the next thing I was on the train to Liverpool. A group of young boys sat on the seat opposite me. They were happy and laughing and nudging each other and doing all the things that simply did not match what was going on inside me. The journey seemed to take forever. I asked myself every question I possibly could and answered it the best way I knew, but the fact was the *Lady Irene*, my son's boat had collided with a Liverpool ferry.

When I arrived at Lime Street, my son Nigel was waiting for me. I have often asked myself but have never actually asked Nigel what brought him to the station, but there he was. He looked strained and pale. I clung to him, 'Where is Carl? Where is Carl?'

'He's fine,' said Nigel. 'He's in hospital suffering from exhaustion, but he'll be fine.'

I learned as we travelled to the hospital that his dear son Arragorn, three years old, had drowned. That Aeneas his brother, aged five, had managed to swim beneath the ferry and up the other side, where he was met by Carl, who was searching, frantically searching. Arragorn was in the hold of Carl's yacht with Annette, Carl's wife, when it struck the ferry. Deep in the water, Annette was clinging to her little boy and a great chain had separated them. She was found a mile down river and given the kiss of life by a fisherman and was now, along with Carl, in hospital suffering from sheer exhaustion. Arragorn had not been found. Apart from Arragorn, Carl's best friend's wife and baby had also perished.

Later, Claremont House was crowded with policemen, divers, press – there were great arguments as to where Arragorn might be found – everyone had a different theory. I heard the phone ringing in the kitchen. I went to answer it. Something I had written was in rehearsal and a voice said, 'Carla darling, do you remember in scene two, that scene where he leaves the office, could you give me a little line for him darling, a sort of 'out' line – it seems a bit empty.' I mechanically sat down in the kitchen, wrote the line and phoned it back. It was quite a long time before I actually recalled this strange incident.

It is hard to have to remember the terrible times which followed. The mother and baby were never found. Carl and Annette were called to the police station several times to identify clothes found in the river. None of them was Arragorn's – but one night, they were. Arragorn was found three months later. Annette had been devastated and was still ill. Carl had changed completely, no longer the laughing man I knew. After the accident, the media were our worst enemy. They kept taking sneak pictures of me and of Carl or Nigel, standing by the riverside waiting for news. The papers were full of these and it was all part of the kind of nightmare that follows a story like this.

When Arragorn was found, because of the situation, he was basically just a tiny body bag. Claremont became a place of quiet grieving. Carl and Annette dealt with all that followed the best way they could. Carl has never spoken of it since. Annette, however, who always spoke profoundly, seemed to take from her experience something spiritual and once or twice she has been able to explain to me how she felt when she was in the water and saw her little boy floating away from her. Her comfort seems to come from that thing some of us experience when we have lost somebody, the feeling that they have never really left us. Nigel had disappeared and gone to stay with a friend because he was emotionally unequipped to take it all on board. My mother hardly spoke, as if nothing had happened. She came out of her sorrow in her own way, and it was probably six months after that that we all nearly became ourselves again. But in each one of us something had gone, and one of the things which had gone was a little boy, smiling and with his brown arms folded, standing on the table and saying 'I'm going to say a poem'.

At some point during this tragic time, the BBC had rung me asking for more *Bread*. Now I was ready to pick up my pen and write again. I loved doing *Bread*. The cast were so young and so funny and, as before, there was never one dull moment in rehearsals. The character Joey became an idol and Peter Howitt couldn't walk through the streets without attracting a huge deluge of activity. Young girls fell in love with him and older ones claimed to have had a son just like him. Having found a typical street in Liverpool, with typical people living in it, the series had become associated with that street and now we were back. Crowds were gathered to watch us and waited expectantly to see Grandad charge out of the house shouting 'Piss off the lot of you', or Aveline struggling up the street in her tight clothes and high heels, or Mrs Boswell rushing into the street shouting 'She is a tart', or Joey, just going to his car – a picture of pride and dignity, opening the door and getting into it with perfect grace.

The highlight of all highlights was when we gained permission to film our Christmas show in Rome. We travelled each morning from the hotel in a great bus, which seemed to be made of windows. We journeyed through the new Rome, the poor Rome and the wonderful pillars, stones and statues of the old Rome. Our destination was a sort of plateau, which overlooked another part of Rome. The story was a complicated one – the family had decided to go to Rome, each member carrying a memory of a previous visit. We see little shots of the memories interwoven with how things in their lives were now. It made a funny and touching story. The success of *Bread* can be measured by the fact that even when we were in Rome we were followed by the British and Italian press everywhere we went.

The accolades continued – the cast were invited to perform a sketch for the Royal Variety Show and later the play of *Bread* had a successful summer season in Bournemouth before being taken to the West End. These were the very best days.

Chapter **18**

MATRIMONIAL

I decided it was time that I attended to my divorce. I took it to a brilliant solicitor in Liverpool, well known by all for his stinging dialogue. His name was Rex Makin, a strongly Jewish man with a need to tell it how it is. I arrived at his office in Dale Street, and, after climbing some fairly tatty stairs, I reached the reception. It was set in the middle of a long narrow passageway that was crowded with people and prams and babies and even a mongrel dog. The air was thick with that wonderful Liverpool accent as it rose above the sound of crying, coughing, dummy sucking and discontented kids. Without looking at me, the girl at the desk said, 'Property, finance or matrimonial?'

I adjusted my newly acquired dark glasses and whispered, 'Matrimonial.'

'Over there,' she said, pointing in the air, and I managed to sit next to a woman who kept murmuring, 'Oh, my back,' and then 'Oh God, where's our Kevin now?'

Kevin, who was about three years old, was just completing the removal of a door knob from one of the other doors. 'Kevin, come here. Wait till I get you 'ome. Put that back,' she shouted.

Another lady joined in. Her child was yelling and pulling at her scarf because he wanted to remove the door knob. 'Shurrup,' she said, 'and wipe yer nose.' A lady on the other side of me said, 'Would you pick up me baby's dummy, luv, me back's killing me?'

This was the very stuff I loved about Liverpool. The earthy truth; the uninhibited display of hardship and disappointment.

My name was called, or should I say yelled – 'Mrs Lane, please. Over there.' The receptionist nodded towards another door. I knocked and someone shouted, 'Come in.'

Mr Makin was standing with one foot on a chair and his trouser leg rolled up to his knee. He pointed to what looked like a rash on his leg. 'See that,' he ordered.

I looked, 'Yes.'

'That is a rash.'

'Yes.'

'Do you know how I got that rash?'

'Er, no.'

'By seeing people like you who come to me with their life's problems and expect me to solve them.' He clicked his fingers. 'Just like that.'

He pointed to a chair. 'Sit down.' His leg now safely tucked away, he strolled towards the chair opposite me. 'So, what can I do for you?'

I was not inhibited by this strange greeting; in fact, I drew comfort from it. This man, I thought, is different, human even. I said, 'Er, it's a divorce. I want a divorce.'

The questions came back like a shotgun.

'Is he violent?'

'No,' I said.

'Is he mean?'

'No.'

'Is he having an affair?'

'No'

'Does he physically abuse you?'

'No.'

'Does he in any manner or way give you good reason to leave him?'

I was confused. Eric did not fit into any of those categories. I attempted to explain.

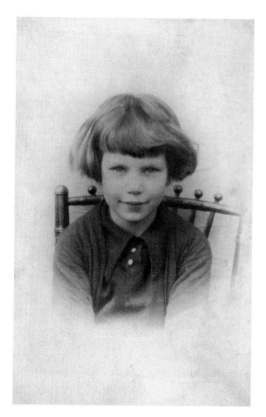

Me aged eight.

My Father and me in the days of the bungalow.

My father, one week before he died.

Myra and me. The very first pictures taken when *The Liver Birds* started.

Me – the final day of the divorce preceedings – my mother close behind.

My mother at Claremont house.

Pathetic picture! Myra and me at the
height of fame!

Me, writing. Zoffany Heights.

Very early days of *The Liver Birds*. Polly, Nerys and me in front.

Eric and me at the top of the Eiffel Tower.

My brother Ramon and myself – Claremont.

Carl, Nigel and me in Liverpool on the day of my OBE.

Me – discovering that I was being photographed!

Me, with Liverpool University students after telling them about the art of TV writing.

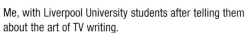

Linda, Paul and me filming
Bread in Liverpool.

Michael Winner, Paul, Linda and me – party at
Broadhurst Manor.

Linda and me – happiest days.

Liverpool. Linda and me during the filming of *Bread*, when she and Paul had a part in the show.

Paul, Linda and me outside Broadhurst Manor. The best photograph taken with Linda.

Me in Zoffany house with Igor – my first wolfhound.

Igor the 3rd with Shy – my dogs of today in Broadhurst Manor.

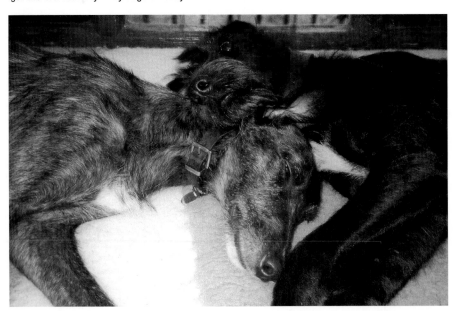

'He, he, I . . .'

'Well, is it he, or I?' he snapped.

'It's that I just don't want to be married to him anymore.'

He took out a large white handkerchief and wiped his forehead. 'I see, I see. Have you spoken to him about it?'

'Yes.'

He stood up.

'So.'

He paced the floor, tucked his fingers in the top pocket of his waist-coat. 'Finance, what about finances?'

'I am reasonably well off,' I explained. 'He has been made redundant. I think he has some money. We have a large house.'

'Is that all? A large house.'

'I have a house in London.'

'And who bought these houses?'

I didn't like saying it but it was the truth. 'I did.'

He sat down again. 'Something else to put in your *Liver Birds*, eh?'

I didn't expect that, I thought I was totally incognito.

'Er, yes, I suppose so.'

He leapt up again. 'Right, let's get down to business.'

He paced the floor, throwing all kinds of questions at me and not waiting for any answers. He was an agitated, obviously clever, no-messing-around man who knew what he was doing. 'I'll get in touch with you when I must,' he finally said, and I left his office, feeling that I was in good hands.

Back at Claremont, sitting by a big log fire in my mother's part of the house, I told her word for word what had happened. I paced about the floor, imitating him and every word he spoke, and I threw my arms about just the way he did. My mother listened intently and then, in the sweetest voice, she said, 'So what did he say?'

I knew that the following days were going to be upsetting. Eric sat, pale and sombre when I told him that I had seen my solicitor. I had prepared myself for a huge emotional scene, but his response shocked me. 'You are the guilty party,' he said, 'and you will pay dearly for this.'

I thought he meant emotionally and I expected that. He went on, 'I want half the value of Claremont for a start, or maybe Claremont itself. I've already seen my solicitor, so let's get on with it.' He left the room and the house slamming several doors.

I went back to my mother.

'I've just had a row with Eric,' I said.

'I'm sorry,' she said, 'that I didn't hear everything you said, but I've lost my hearing aid again. It was in that little black dish.' And I thought, 'Oh no, not that fucking little black dish again.'

The next few months were almost overwhelming. I had been commissioned to write more *Bread* which was fine, but the paperwork, the questions and the endless saga of my affidavit clashed with the writing of my scripts. I was becoming run down. The BBC were depending on me now and had in fact put me on a special contract which although meant that I had to write a certain amount of scripts a year, unlike the previous leisurely contract, was financially exciting. My impending divorce, however, had crept into the gossip columns and Eric had taken to talking to them about his love and faithfulness, leaving me wide open for attack.

Rita Tushingham was still going through her divorce at the time. We spent each day sitting in Harrods' restaurant eating everything they put before us and exchanging our experiences with our husbands, barristers and affidavits. Rita was a great help to me; her sense of humour always emerged and saved us from despair. I remember one morning, as we entered Harrods, I asked one of the assistants what time it was? She answered in a hugely posh accent, "There's a clock on the wall, modam" and ever since, each time Rita and I meet, I say, "Could you tell me the time, please?" and Rita in her finest snobby accent replies, "There's a fucking clock on the fucking wall, modam"!

Chapter 19

FEAR

During the next few months, I managed to get a series of *Bread* written. Somehow, it flowed from my pen as if I had nothing whatever to do with it. Now and then, the flow was interrupted by visits from 'Him', and now and then we managed to do normal things together, like having dinner in a restaurant without worrying about being seen together. Once, during a lull in rehearsals, we nipped off to a little hotel in some remote place. All was going well until one morning we were coming down the main staircase and right at the bottom of the stairs, on a large red sofa, sat three actresses with whom he had often worked. With alarming dexterity, we parted – he moving to the right-hand stair rail and me clinging to the left as if we were not together. I walked through to the main lounge, there to have a quiet coffee, while he was besieged by the three ladies – 'Darling, how lovely to see you', 'Darling, you look wonderful', the word 'darling' being to and fro-ed like a tennis ball and finally, the endless hugging and kissing, which I had not yet grown used to. He joined me at the door, somewhat covered with lipstick, and we quietly slipped out of the hotel feeling as though we had escaped from a possible catastrophe.

Shortly after this event, I was stricken with a pain and my doctor suggested that I needed to have my appendix out. 'No bother,' I thought;

in fact, I had begun to think of this even as a 'rest'. As I lay on the table outside the operating theatre, the anaesthetist smiled down at me and said the usual thing, 'I'm going to give you an injection to put you to sleep, just relax now and breathe deeply', which I did. I counted to three and then, for some reason, I wasn't able to say four or five. There was a kind of haziness. I could hear everything that was going on, the thin clatter of instruments against the steel table, the occasional greeting between the man who was attending to me and another passing doctor. And then suddenly my legs felt very heavy, I mean, really heavy. I couldn't move them and almost immediately the same feeling travelled to my arms. 'I'd better tell him,' I thought, 'just in case.' But although he was only inches away from my reach and I could hear him busily engaged in rearranging things on the steel table, I couldn't move my arms or my legs or any part of my body. I tried to raise my head, anything to attract his attention but I couldn't lift it. I felt as if I were a huge, heavy, fallen log. Strangely enough, I was not yet frightened. I kept thinking that this was some new drug and that soon I would go to sleep or the doctor would turn round and see me. But then I couldn't close my eyes or my mouth – everything was frozen.

Now I was panicking. I had no way of telling anybody what was happening. People were passing and having conversations with the doctor but no one noticed my plight and then, worst of all, my lungs refused to move. They sat like a great stone on my chest and I could neither breathe in nor out. I cannot explain what it was like. Whatever the injection had been I knew now that it was not the right one. I struggled desperately to make my chest move, I felt as though I wanted to burst all over – my brain became confused and I could no longer remember where I was and it grew dark. Finally, there was a loud, drum-like banging in my head, getting slower and slower. A little piece of my brain thought, 'I'm suffocating.' Somewhere in the deep black, I heard a distant voice. It was a man's voice, not the doctor's. It was alarmed, 'Jesus Christ,' it said, 'Jesus.' And everything went black. I still believe that I died at that moment.

The following morning, I found myself in a private ward. They had put cot rails round my bed and I could see many white coats standing round me. I still couldn't see very well, but at least I could breathe.

'How are you?' said a gentle voice.

'Fine.'

'Any pain?'

'No.'

And then 'I can't see.'

Silence for a moment.

'We've put you where it's quiet,' said another voice.

'Thank you,' I said.

'Your appendix has been removed. All is well. There were no problems.'

I tried to say 'thank you', but it wouldn't come.

I don't remember any more. I think I probably fell asleep. I disclosed this story to a doctor friend, who came in to visit me. He was very concerned. 'This,' he said, 'was curare.' He was very grave. 'We give it to stop you flinching during surgery but it's obvious they hadn't given you an airway beforehand. You were suffocating. It's a good job they finally noticed.' From that day on I have been seriously claustrophobic.

Not long after, I was watching a television programme about animals in Africa. It showed men hunting with darts and the chosen animal running and running, becoming slower and slower, and then falling and dragging itself and finally lying still. That was curare, and that is man.

Chapter **20**

CHANGES

Shortly after *Bread* finished, commanding as many as twenty million viewers, things began to change at the BBC. Computers had arrived, writers could no longer just turn up and ask for the Head of Comedy and then be greeted with, 'Hello darling, what are you going to write for us next?' Heads of departments became unreachable. If you were lucky, your script might get a reading and often this resulted in a rejection.

A new kind of comedy was being born. It was a different format, a different language even, throwing some viewers into a state of confusion. We were galloping towards something very new, and the middle-aged generation was slowly being squeezed out. I decided to try and write for the stage, and after spending almost a year bashing out an hour-long comedy drama called *Our Doris*, when it was finally accepted, it was so changed that I did not recognise it, and I took it back. I then decided to write a book and called it *Instead of Diamonds*. It was published and a week afterwards I was completely exhausted having been dragged all over the country in a car to be interviewed at radio stations from up North to down South. After two days of this, I refused to do anything more. This was very foolish of me. The book got good reviews but because I did not complete the duties expected of an author, it was not widely publicised. My attitude aggravated the publishers and I escaped with just enough money to see me through for a few more months. I was also lucky enough to be receiving money from other situation comedies I had written, namely *Solo*, *The Mistress*, *Screamin'*, *Luv* and *Searchin'* (for ITV). These series had a normal TV life, not to be compared with the fever of *Liver Birds*, *Butterflies* and *Bread*. I turned to trying to write a different kind of comedy. This resulted in *I Woke Up One Morning*.

At this time, Michael Grade was in charge. He was a special man with the BBC's future first on his mind. He read the scripts and loved them and I remember him saying, 'These may not be the funniest scripts, Carla, but they are thoughtful and different and I'm going to show them', which he did, on BBC2. In those days, BBC2 was not watched by many people and *I Woke Up One Morning* sank slowly into nothingness, but even so Michael still held his love of the series. Shortly afterwards, he left the BBC, but it is comforting to know that, after a long time, he has now returned.

Now, about 'Him'. There was no doubt that in some curious way we loved each other, although neither of us would use that word 'love'. It seemed to sit inside us – sort of waiting. We were hanging on to a thread that stretched between us, waiting for fate. It reminded me of the rats in the yard having a tug of war with a piece of bread and along comes a cockerel and snatches it. Neither of them ends up with any of it.

An American producer got in touch with me asking me if I would go to Los Angeles to write scripts there. It so happened that 'He' and I had just had a very serious quarrel, the quarrel of all quarrels. It was about nothing and everything. We were like two kids – he pulled my hair so I pulled his. As I stormed out of his flat and drove off into the dark night, I felt a secret delight in the idea of pissing off to America without telling him, and within two weeks I found myself flying first class to Los Angeles. I never liked flying and all I can recall in between the lavish food and unbelievable comfort and attention is my vigil by the window. Most of what I saw was spectacular, strips of flat land turning quickly into white, mountain peaks rearing up and then dropping down into great crevices. There were silver rivers cutting their way towards a worrying sea and in the distance red, rock cliffs. Other journeys I had made to other countries had never seemed so dramatic. It was all blue and white and I kept imagining what it must be like to plummet downwards. Eventually, I fell asleep during a very boring film. I awoke when the gentleman beside me fell into a deep sleep and his head ended up on my shoulder.

I kept trying to think about the people I had left behind, but in the end all I could think about was my dog, Egor, sitting rigid, the tip of his tail beating against the ground and the thing I love best, those all-knowing eyes. I discovered it is much easier to leave people than to leave your dog.

I arrived at the poshest hotel which looked like a big slice of wedding cake. My suite had four rooms, two bathrooms, three televisions, four balconies and what seemed like hundreds of windows, some of which overlooked the town itself, others overlooked mountains and desert, another overlooked the Hollywood sign and a smaller one overlooked the balcony of a block of flats where I noticed that there was a large parrot cage on a table which had a cover over it. On a table in the sitting room was an enormous gold box of chocolates and enough flowers to fill a cemetery.

Within moments I was informed that (I can only remember his first name) Roger was waiting for me downstairs in the lounge. As I went down the ornate staircase from the lifts, I kept wishing that fate had taken me to Spain or Italy, anywhere but Los Angeles. I knew immediately that I was not going to like it. Roger wanted me to work with him on an American comedy. This seemed very exciting and I agreed to do it. I promised a first script, and immediately a large amount of dollars was deposited in my bank. It didn't end there: every Wednesday of the seven Wednesdays that I stayed there, somebody arrived at the hotel with an envelope containing a thousand dollars – they called it spending money.

Here I should be telling you how marvellous it was, how lucky I was, how rich I was becoming, but I never could stand the sunshine. Los Angeles seemed to be full of people who were brown, thin and full of yoghurt. Dogs were not allowed to walk on the pavements, everything was pristine, everybody was dressed too beautifully. One breakfast was enough to last me for a fortnight. Everybody was so charming. I was longing for something ordinary, something cool, a bed that was not built for seven others and a bathroom that had a tap that didn't quite turn off.

Roger called me again. He said that my car was waiting for me outside if I would like to drive around and take a look at Los Angeles. I sent a message back: 'Yes, please. Take me somewhere, anywhere. Can we get to the North Pole from here?' The enormous limo arrived and I was helped in by a tall, blonde, amazing-looking, young man. He shook my hand. 'I'm the driver,' he said, 'we're going to the Aquaria – it's on the coast. Do you like sea monsters?'

'I do,' I said, 'I like all animals.'

'Oh my God, you're not vegetarian are you? This place is crawling with them, oh God no.'

I tried to keep thinking about the proper meeting arranged for the next day, but my eye could not help taking in the wonderful wild countryside, turning now and then into a motorway but suddenly turning back again into a wilderness. There always seemed to be tall trees, huge crimson flowering bushes, the kind that the posh people had back home. There were beautifully tidy, bright green lawns in front of the houses, with pillars, arches, bright, pebbled pathways, heavy wooden doors and always the swimming pool competing with the bluest of skies. 'Oh by the way,' said the driver, 'did I tell you. My name is Rex.'

'Hi Rex,' I said.

'What's it like in Liverpool? I've heard it's a bit jaded, you know what I mean?'

I thought of the tiny streets, little houses with no swimming pools, everything clinging together, each with its little patch of garden and if they were lucky, lawn. I saw toothless grandmas and grandfathers sitting in the parks with their grandchildren. I saw skies hesitating to become blue, I saw rain and traffic jams and tall buildings, large shopping areas, tiny, green parks and Queen Victoria's statue with her sitting beneath a marble arch surrounded by smoke-stained buildings.

'It's great,' I said, 'it's nothing like Los Angeles but it's, it's, it's got a great heart.'

'Wow, great,' he said, 'I like that.'

I was on a 'zig' now about my city.

'And,' I said, 'art and culture and technology and talent . . .'

He interrupted, 'Do they all talk like you?'

I didn't know how to answer that one, so I just laughed.

The Aquaria was sensational; great sharks nosing you through the plate glass. You could see quite plainly their tiny evil-looking eyes and their teeth. Now and then, they would open their mouth as if to boast about its capabilities. There were whales, dolphins, everything to do with water. I was enthralled with the amazing relationship between the keeper and these great animals.

'They should be free,' I murmured, 'they should be free.'

'Free,' said Rex, 'then we would never see them. We would never know anything about them. Gee, you're so English.'

From a special place, obviously reserved for various TV companies, I watched these great creatures leap and drop from and into the water. They had a kind of excitement surrounding them, not the imprisoned look which I had expected. They seemed to like showing off and the relationship between them and their handlers was more than touching.

'Thank you Rex,' I said outside the hotel.

'Thank you Miss Carla,' he said, and then with a grotesque attempt at the Liverpool accent he called after me, 'I'll see yer later, ay then, luv?'

A parcel had arrived for me. It contained a few scripts for me to read. I read one and was filled with dread. The dialogue was light and frothy and jokey, none of the characters were real. 'I can't write this,' I kept muttering to myself, 'I can't write this.'

The couple in the script were supposed to be in love but it was really all jokes. When I wrote about love it was really love and love is painful as well as funny. I was filled with that word which crops up often in this book, fear. 'I'm not clever enough to do these kind of scripts,' I explained to Roger. 'OK, honey,' he said, 'it's no worry. I have some good news for you. Let's have some lunch, the others are waiting.'

The others were six or seven, I forget, but a mixture of producers, writers and God knows what. Roger had booked a room at the hotel for us to lunch in. I was introduced. 'This is Buck, this is Ted, this is Chuck.' And each one said, 'Hi there, nice to meet you.'

In an effort to get my inadequacies over, I said, 'I'm a bit scared. I'm not sure I can write for American television. It's different.'

They all chorused together, 'Oh my God, that Liverpool accent. It's fantastic, it's Beatle time.'

Roger intervened, 'So the good news is, we're going to do *Butterflies*.' A terrible vision flashed before me. I could hear Ben saying 'Gee, I love you honey' to Ria and Ria to Ben saying 'OK, OK, so I get the dress I saw in Freemans'.

My troubled face quickly took on an act of elation. 'Oh Roger, that's fantastic, thank you.'

'Didn't I tell you, didn't I tell you?'

'Oh God,' said one of them, 'I can see it already. A scene where they first meet. He says something like, "You flicked your ash in my trifle". He's doing a sitting down dance now. And she could say, "Oh, I'm so sorry", and she can swap trifles, you know as if she doesn't mind eating ash.'

They all roared. I died inside.

The following morning a big, bright red car was waiting outside the hotel. Someone came towards me, 'Miss Lane?'

'Yes,' I said.

'Care of the studio, ma'am, drive carefully.'

Filled with another kind of dread, I immediately called Rex to come and save me.

After many cups of coffee and bagels with cream cheese, I was persuaded to do just one of the *Butterflies* for them. 'Just one,' I said. They saw the worry on my face. 'Don't be scared,' said Roger, 'you write the script, we'll rewrite it.'

I now found myself in a plush office at the top of Cold Water Canyon. I had decided to try and drive the big red car and I have never been so frightened in my life. On one side of the road up the Canyon was a sheer drop, and the rest was twisting and turning and surprising me at every yard. Other cars impatiently drove behind me beeping their horns. I couldn't pull over to let them pass so we all got to work late. I arrived at the office, which turned out to be a little bungalow, fully furnished, with a typist poised by her machine that printed out every word I spoke. A man introduced himself, 'Hi, I'm Leo, I'm your runner,' he announced.

'Runner? What does that mean?'

'I get your breakfast, I park your car, I get anything you want – bagels are good up here.'

I was bloody sick of bagels by this time.

'Let me introduce you to Mr Miltonberg. A very famous man.'

He was about sixty-five, grey haired, with a pleasant face, a loud voice and brimming over with past successes.

'Hi, Milton Miltonberg,' he said. 'I wrote for Jack Benny.'

'That's wonderful,' I said.

We sat opposite each other. He handed me my first original *Butterflies* script.

'We, Carla,' he said, 'you and I, are going to go over this one, OK?'

'OK,' I murmured.

'Would you like some donuts?' Leo asked.

'Oh yeah,' cried the girl at the machine, 'that's fabulous, that's wild.'

'Thank you Leo,' I said.

'OK, there I go,' and he shot off.

I looked at the typist and said, 'What is your name?'

'I'm Kelly,' she said in an exaggerated southern accent. 'I'm here to type whatever you guys want me to type.'

She flashed her spider-like eyelashes and banged away on the type-writer, her long, bright red fingernails clattering against the metal.

'Now then, Miss Carla,' said Milton, 'this first line said by Ria, OK? She's calling Ben from the hall?'

'Yes,' I said, 'yes.'

'She is calling, "Ben! Ben!"'

'Yes,' I said.

'I'm going to have her shout, "I know you're there honey. Your after-shave just killed the flowers down here."'

I felt it was funny and was relieved. Milton had already written it down and then he changed his mind.

'I think that is funny but not funny enough. She will shout, "Honey, are you there with your aftershave, or did the flowers die a natural death?"'

It was not as bad as I had expected.

Kelly screamed laughing. Now Leo was back with an enormous bag full of hot donuts and what seemed like gallons of coffee. I had gone quiet. 'This is going to be the end of me as a writer,' I thought.

Leo said, 'Something wrong? You OK with the coffee?'

'I'm fine Leo, thank you. I was just looking at that picture on the wall, it's sort of . . .'

He leapt out of his chair. 'You don't like the picture, I'll get you another picture. I'll change all the pictures, they're crap anyway.'

'No, no,' I said, 'it's not that important. If it could just be put on another wall.'

He picked up the phone before I could finish, he dialled and then: 'Hi this is Leo from Radnor. We don't like the pictures, OK. Could we have another set please, OK, thanks.'

He put the phone down.

Kelly said, 'Gee Carla, I love your work, you're so funny.'

I didn't enjoy being called funny. Milton said, 'I wrote for Jack Benny, gee that was funny, that was really funny.'

As we spoke a call came through for me. I heard the words, 'OK, she's right here.' It was 'Him'.

'Hello,' I said.

'Hello, is it a wrong time?'

'No, no, it's fine.'

'Are you OK?'

'Yeah, I'm fine.'

'I've sent you a parcel, did you get it?'

'Not yet, no.'

'All right.' There was a pause. 'How was the flight, scary? I don't like flying you know that, but we all do it, don't we?'

'We were late.'

'I know. I saw you leaving.' Pause. 'I'll talk to you again, take care, bye.'

'Bye.'

I put the phone down. For a fleeting moment I realised he had, in spite of our terrible quarrel, been on the terrace and watched the plane leave. I was interrupted by Milton.

'Honey,' he said, 'this is America, USA, the great country; we are not little England. Our sense of humour is less, less . . .' He had difficulty in thinking of how to put it.

'Funny,' I found myself thinking.

'Refined,' he said, 'that's it refined.' And then he confidentially whispered, 'I worked for Jack Benny. You know that guy?'

'No, no, I don't, but he was very funny. He had some good jokes.'

He cried out, 'Not jokes honey, gags. He makes gags and a hundred per cent good ones and your script is going to be even funnier.'

I fell very quiet after that. The whole project lost its interest. As we went through the script, I couldn't bear to see *Butterflies* being executed. I couldn't possibly go through a whole series simply killing my own work. I went to see Roger.

'Come on honey,' he said, 'let me drive you around. We'll talk that way.'

As we slowly cruised along the wide roads, flanked by the greenest grass and behind these great pink and white houses, each one looking like an iced bun, he said, 'You know honey,' pointing to one of these, 'this could be yours.'

I winced at the thought.

He pointed again: 'See that one, Lucille Ball lives there. I'm telling you honey, it could be God damn you.'

I decided that I should let the scripts go and get on a plane home. I said quietly, 'I'm not happy here, Roger. I don't like my scripts being changed.' I raised my voice and was nearly crying, 'I mean changed! They are no longer mine. Milton's name should be there, not mine.'

He was silent; I was riddled with guilt. I had been shown such hospitality. I was being paid so much money. I tried another way.

'I miss my dog,' I whispered.

He came back quickly, 'You want a dog, I'll get you a dog.'

'I want *my* dog.'

'Where is he? God damn Liverpool – I'll get him from there.'

Before I could answer he was pointing to another huge white mansion: 'See that honey, it could be yours.'

I just uttered a big sigh.

'OK, OK, so you want to go home, but have you heard of the word "contract", have you?'

'I signed to go over *Butterflies* with you and I will. I can do it from home, we can do it on the phone.'

He was losing his grace.

'But honey, am I supposed to fly to England every five minutes to work on the script?'

The tears had reached my eyes by now.

'But that's the trouble,' I said, 'everybody is working on the script. There is no need for me. You can do what you like with them. I want to go home.'

There was a long silence as he drove slowly, stopping now and then, not saying anything but wanting me to survey the property that he had stopped in front of. Then he said, 'You like the hotel?'

'Yes, yes, thank you, it's great.'

'You want to move?'

'No, no, it's fine.'

'How about if I moved you to . . .?'

'It's fine, just let's finish the script and then I'll go. I'm sorry, I'm truly sorry.'

When I arrived at the hotel, there was a parcel waiting for me – it was from 'Him'. It was a tape of a Tchaikovsky violin concerto – we had often listened to this together.

The script, now miraculously completed, the American producer had laid on a going home party to be held in a restaurant in Santa Monica. I was very moved by the lengths these people were going to please me and guilt kept visiting me over and over again. The place was packed with people who were involved in the *Butterflies* project. They were all charming: 'Gee, I'm so sorry you're going. *Butterflies* is beautiful.'

In the middle of all this praise, I noticed a large tank on the counter. It was filled with lobsters. People were coming into the restaurant, pointing to one and the chosen fish was taken out into the kitchen at the back. I started staring at the tank. My mind was working overtime. There were five lobsters left. Milton came up to me. 'Do you want one honey?' And before I could speak he had called to the producer, 'Can we do one of these for Carla?'

'No, no, no,' I protested. 'I don't eat animals.'

'These are not animals, honey, these are fish.'

'I don't eat fish,' I whispered.

The producer said, as everybody gathered round, 'OK, OK, everybody calm now. We have a problem.'

'I'm sorry,' I whimpered.

'No, honey, not you, you're not the problem. The lobsters are the problem.'

'They should be left in the sea,' I said pathetically, and I know how foolish I sounded.

'She's right, she's right, the lobsters should be left in the sea.'

He called the manager of the restaurant, pointed to the lobsters. 'Could you put these guys on my bill please.'

The Manager almost bowed to him. 'Did you want them to be prepared now?'

'No, no, I'll see to it. Just charge me, OK.'

The producer called the runner. 'Put these guys back in the sea, OK?'

The runner looked bewildered. 'Now?'

'Now,' said the producer, 'it's only two miles away and we have a serious problem here.'

He rushed me to a table and sat me down. 'There,' he said, 'relax, OK. There'll be no more dead lobsters, OK?'

'OK,' I whispered and the party continued.

Such kind, charming, irritatingly nice people.

At the hotel, I literally bumped into the British scriptwriter, Johnny Speight, who wrote that lovely series *Till Death Us Do Part*. I had several hours to go before my flight home, so we decided to go to a place called

Little Venice, situated on the wide sands of the ocean. Here was the American version of our Portobello Road, except that it dealt with people and not objects. There were rows of small plots of land, all cordoned off from each other and on each plot the devotee of a certain act. The Strongest Man in LA, the fattest couple in LA and, oh God, were they fat. There was the cowboy who wielded a whip and sang and yodelled to a record; a lady who cavorted around on a wooden horse and was catapulted off it at every moment; a man who specialised in singing off key; a weight lifter with a black, shiny body, muscles like mountains and tight short shorts, which had embroidered across his genitalia 'love thing'; a man dressed in rags, playing one song on an accordion and a different song altogether at the same time. This was the America I enjoyed most. I really didn't want to leave. We had a nice meal and Johnny told me that he loved being in America. I decided not to disillusion him. We hugged and off I went back to the hotel.

The American version of *Butterflies* was recorded not long after. I was flown by Concord to New York and then on to Los Angeles, to be there on the night of recording and found myself with a strangely loving feeling towards all those people who once made me want to go home, but as for the programme, it was awful. I learned later that the man who played the lead role in *Butterflies* in America died suddenly two days after the recording. It was hard for me to take in because on the night we had sat together exchanging our views on life.

This was not the end of America – I made five more trips in an attempt to provide them with an acceptable script, but they were fruitless journeys. My very English style of writing could not be easily adapted, not by me anyway.

The producer did everything to please me. I hated the lavish hotels, so he invited me to stay in his house, which was built on a hill overlooking Los Angeles. He had five amazing Husky dogs. I kept saying to him, 'They are fantastic'. His reply was, 'You want five dogs, I'll get you five dogs.' He was a lovely man and when he drove me to the airport, I expected him to look at the jumbo jet and say, 'This could be yours Carla'.

One day, Carl called me from England. He had read that a small island off the coast of Wales was for sale. The lady who owned it was being criticised because the deer on the island had died, all but one.

'It's fabulous, Mother. It's only small, but it's full of wildlife – it's fantastic.'

'Buy it,' I said, 'let's buy it.'

I knew as I said it that earning so much money was not making me a better person. I was becoming irresponsible. The island was called St Tudwells East. It was situated about two miles off the Welsh coast, and on the other side was the never-ending ocean. Because of my work I was not able to go and see the island immediately. Carl rang me again and told me about a cottage for sale overlooking the island.

'Buy it,' I said.

It was a lovely June day when I finally did visit my island. Carl, Nigel and I clambered up a rough pathway, which pushed itself in between great rocks and banks of wild flowers. At the top, a once-upon-a-time church stood. Its stones were old and cracked but the place itself was filled with mystery. It rose high over one end of the island so that you could look out across the ocean. What a beautiful place it was. The entire island was covered with nesting birds; it was impossible to walk anywhere without placing your feet carefully between nests. Beaks snapped up at us and guarding wings flapped all around us. We were obviously not welcome by the residents and it was frustrating not to be able to explain that we would not harm them. In an effort not to disturb them, we decided to leave quickly.

Outside the little church, there was a small piece of land which was fenced off and to our amazement there she was, a previously unnoticed doe, giving birth to her young, and lying beside her the carcass of her mate. All the rest had been removed but the male looked as if he was just asleep, his hide was beautiful, and it was impossible to imagine that he had been dead for many months. We all felt that this lifelike image of him had helped her through her pregnancy and giving birth. Quietly and quickly, we left, but Nigel had taken a short film of it and it was shown on television that same evening.

Chapter 21

ACCOLADES

I arrived back in London from Los Angeles one late afternoon and was met by 'Him'. I wanted to run to him and consume him but I knew it would frighten him to death.

'Did you have a good time?'

'Yes, well sort of, it's all too loud for me, too fast.'

I sat in the front seat of his car and before he started the engine he looked at me and smiled. I phoned Marna and Len and told them that I had arrived and that we were going for a meal and that I would see them soon. We drove straight to his flat.

All was well at Zoffany House. Marna and Len as usual had kept everything in order, including all the animals residing there. Having picked up each cat and given them a kiss, which being cats none of them enjoyed, a little cuddle of the guinea pig and the rabbit, and Bell my faithful pigeon and a rough and tumble with Egor, it was time to go and see Helicopter. This was a little thrush that I had picked up two years before in the garden. He was totally crippled and could not walk properly but bounced up and down, up and down. For some reason, it never seemed to bother him. I nursed him for many days but he never regained his ability to walk properly like a bird. I truly loved the devotion of this little bird and after greeting all the larger animals, I rushed to the aviary to see him. I took with me some grapes, his favourite thing and the moment he saw me he bounced and bounced towards me. I picked him up, cuddled him, put him down and he was eating his grape as I left the aviary, and then as I neared the door I felt something beneath my foot. He had followed me and now he was lifeless on the floor. It was an agonising moment. I took him into another room, closed the door and found myself weeping, not just ordinary weeping but huge desperate sobs. This little bird had shown more concern, more love and more celebration of that love than any human being I had known and now he was gone and I had killed him. It haunted me for weeks and months and I still think of him – Helicopter, my crazy little thrush, as I called him.

Eric had been living away from Claremont for some time and the family had settled into a more peaceful atmosphere, instead of having to listen to the eternal drama of our parting. Nevertheless, guilt visited me again. I began to feel rather useless to everybody. My family had been getting on with their marriages, births, ups and downs, and I had become so tangled up in my own affairs that I had allowed the values of family life to slip by. I think they had all guessed about my relationship with 'Him', but I thought that it was now time for them to actually meet him. He was not fazed by the suggestion which amazed me and he came to stay in Claremont House for just a few days. My sons and their wives liked him and I could see there would be no family upsurge. My mother adored him the way she adored Eric. 'So what do you intend?' was the question she asked me. I couldn't answer her because I didn't know. 'I think he doesn't want a fuss,' I explained. 'He is a private person and I have learned to be the same.'

She threw up her hands, 'You mean you're going to go around secretly?'

'Yes.'

'Why?'

'Because I think that's the right way for us. No one in the BBC knows and we don't want the bother of it all yet.'

She looked at me again with those intense eyes. 'That's not normal,' she said. 'You're divorced now, you have a right, you have nothing to hide. Are you sure he hasn't?'

I explained, 'Well of course he hasn't anything to hide. Why should he?'

'It doesn't sound like you – all this secrecy.'

And as she went on and on, I found myself wishing that she had lost her hearing aid.

One day, I was walking my dog in the grounds surrounding the old church near Zoffany House. I always carried a little notebook with me to jot down notes of all kinds. On this particular day, I had thought of a very good idea for another series. So I took out my little notebook and leaned on a nearby tomb to write it down. It was very old and although it was tall the sides were covered with weeds. After making my notes, I parted the weeds and there I could see something written – now I was intrigued. And there it was, the word 'Zoffany'. I was leaning on the very tomb of the man who had lived and died in the house in which I now lived. This link appealed to me so much that I began to write scripts while sitting with my back to his tomb overlooking the vast green patch where my dog played happily with other dogs. I had seen Zoffany's paintings at Buckingham Palace when I received my OBE. I had read a little about him when I purchased the house – sometimes, when I wandered through the Marble Hall, I wondered where he had sat and worked, and now here I was, sitting and working by his tomb. Already the writer in me was, without my permission, gathering a spooky little story together but I didn't allow it to flourish – I preferred the story the way it was.

Chapter 22

PARTING

One day, my sons called me urgently and told me that my mother was not very well – she kept being sick. The doctor had called it an hiatus hernia, which he said was not dangerous and would pass. I drove straight to Liverpool.

My mother was sitting in her usual chair, with the television on and she was passing her wonderfully sharp comments as usual, this time about the Pope who was making a dramatic speech.

'Go on, you silly man, poncing about in a frock, waving your arms about and pretending to bless everybody – only God can do that.'

Her humour never left her, even when she was being taken to hospital in an ambulance. She looked at me and remarked, 'You've got your father's eyes, a pity you didn't inherit my face.' Then she would smile that wide, toothy smile which transformed her into a woman less than half her age.

I had been sitting by my mother's bedside for three days and three nights. They kept telling me that this hiatus hernia was manageable and that soon she would be better. On the third evening, I drove quickly home, only ten minutes away, to have a bath, change my clothes, but before I could get in the car to go back, the hospital called me and said, 'Your mother has taken a turn for the worse.' I knew instantly that what they meant was that she was dead. I don't know why I knew it, and when I arrived on the ward it was true. Her eyes were half open and her lovely slender hands were relaxed and resting on her body, and on her finger was her wedding ring, another ring which my father had given her, and on her other hand a ring that I had bought her on one of our happy, laughing days touring the city, me with my bag full of money buying everything we saw.

I can't remember quite how I reacted. The sister put her arm round me and accompanied me off the ward. During the short journey home, I was asking the question – 'Why did she die so quickly?

'No sugar for me' were her last words, just before I left. She wasn't ready to die. My whole world was sent spinning with grief. The one I had so much in common with, enjoyed so much, loved so much, had gone.

My brother, Ramon, was standing beside me. We were in the Chapel of Rest, and we were gazing silently down at Hive, the name the family always called her. I found myself smiling inside when I thought of the wonderfully funny things she used to say. Her eyes were slightly open and they still shone. Ramon looked pale and shocked. We began to talk about all the strange little things she did, like the time we bought her an electric kettle because we felt that the gas was too dangerous, but she put her electric kettle on the gas and sat gazing at the television as it melted all over the stove.

'No more burning the kettle for you, young lady,' said Ramon. We forced a smile.

'And what about your hearing aid?' I said. 'Where is that young lady?'

And in unison my brother and I said, 'Oh it's in the little black dish.'

We both laughed, but really we wanted to scream.

Here I must say more about my brother. Ramon is a very special person; his deadpan sense of humour never rests and, sitting on his large settee in the house in which he and his wife Dorothy began their life together, he rules the entire family. When he was younger, like my father, he went to sea, and, like my father, he finally came ashore. He has always held a most important job, all to do with ships. How I love to hear him when he answers his phone: 'Hello,' he says, 'this is the Prince speaking.'

And somewhere in the conversation he would suddenly ask, 'Why am I so handsome?' I don't see enough of my brother.

When my brother and I were four and five years old and lived in Liverpool, the biggest thrill each year was that when my father was home from sea, he and my mother would take us to London, the major event being feeding the pigeons in Trafalgar Square. It was the only time that my brother and I could actually have contact with living creatures. They climbed on our shoulders and on our heads; they fluttered all around us. Hundreds of cameras were clicking all day long and the soul of it all was the little man who sold peanuts. Not every parent could afford to buy a carton of peanuts, so the birds were never overfed. Had this idea not been destroyed, there would have been no problems in the square, but the sudden disappearance of the peanut man triggered the animal welfare people into a 'Save the Pigeon' motion, and what happened next was predictable – bags and bags of grain were strewn around the square, as the frustration of the future of these well loved birds caused compassionate people to rise up and, in a word, overfeed. This meant more and more birds, not only the resident ones but visiting birds from other parts of London, which in turn meant more and more young and it became a place that was so packed it was impossible to walk between them. If there had been deep thinking people in the powers that be, they would have seen this and realised that the little peanut man was the instigator of order in the Square, but instead they blamed the people and the people blamed them and the plight of the pigeon hangs in the balance.

Another phone call from 'Him'. It was probably to tell me that he was bursting with love and admiration for me, could not live without me, and wanted to carry me off and keep me from the rest of the world.

'Hello,' I said.

'I have been thinking (he was going to admit that he adored me). How would you like to go to America?'

I wanted to say, 'I've been to America, can't we go somewhere else?' but I said, 'It sounds good – why?'

'Well, I thought I might go there.'

Well, go on, say something to make me feel wanted.

'And I also thought that you might like to come with me.'

Oh, for God's sake, why don't you admit it? You haven't got anyone else to go with you.

'Actually Jennifer (he fancies her, I know he does) asked me if I would like to go with her, but I said it wasn't convenient to leave right now, and then I thought I really would like to make that trip, so I thought of you.'

Well, here's what I thought: 'You are a lying bastard,' I thought, 'and if you thought that I am going to be here at your command, you thought wrong, so you can fuck off.'

We arrived in Los Angeles in the early morning. It was already too hot for me but I didn't complain. We decided to journey through as much of America as we could, staying at little motels. It was a lovely time. We managed to put aside the nonsense of our relationship and concentrate on being normal, intelligent beings taking a breathless look at a wondrous country. We saw the Grand Canyon yawning its way into the earth, the river, shining like a mirror, flowing deep in its bowels, the ever changing red and gold shadows which hung over the great rocks moving restlessly, suddenly plunging them into darkness and then slowly delivering them light. Great black spiders wandered across the stones and disappeared into the yellow flowers that grew in the crevices. Things flew and buzzed around us; everywhere we turned or looked was awesome. Further now into little towns – men wearing cowboy hats, neckerchiefs, chewing gum, riding horses, being John Wayne. Old cars, bars, cafés, nut-brown grandmothers sitting outside flaking painted doors, children – dark, lithe, soprano voices, the whitest teeth, never ending smiles – happy.

Later, we sat in a small café watching the pelicans diving into the sea, disappearing and searing back through the water with a great fish in their beaks. And then we were back on the endless, tree-lined roads, with the crimson sun sinking so low that it looked as though it was actually basking at the end of the road itself. There were times in the cloak of the desert, with nothing to see but cacti, nothing to hear but the odd little sound of odd little insects, more yellow flowers and now and then a creature – never before have you seen him and he moves so fast you are left without knowledge of him.

At night, we would sit in a huge wooden bed watching American television in a little motel, with packets of liquorice allsorts and bottles of pop. The ordinariness of it was much more exciting than the many other things we had done.

One day 'He' and I did manage to behave like a normal couple. We sat outside a house for sale by the river in Chiswick. We talked about how nice it was, how lovely it must be to live in, we even almost decided to buy it. There were a few moments of happy babbling about how we would do the garden, how we would decorate it, how I would have my dog, my cats, my birds, my rabbits and my guinea pigs – his smile faded, and we spiralled downwards.

Chapter **23**

SANCTUARY

Now my life was about to take a different turn. In the early 1990s, I began to look elsewhere for something to do other than writing. The plight of animals had always reached me but I was always too busy for anything but my work. With time to think, I realised that I should follow my 'other person' and do something different and useful. London did not seem the right place to start my new venture – it called for the country-side – green things, wild life, birds in trees and grazing sheep. I started to look for a little cottage set in such a place. There was however, a huge problem. I had been paying someone to look after ten horses that I had rescued. The people who were caring for them could not do it any longer. 'That's all right,' I thought, 'I'll buy a little cottage with grazing ground and stables.' I put this thought to 'Him' carefully, softly, lovingly, and ended by saying, 'You can come too, if you like.'

'I'm not like you,' he said, 'I have never wanted to actually live in the countryside, although I keep dragging you out there at weekends. But my world is here, in London.'

I was not surprised and I was not angry.

'I'm not keen on horses anyway – they are big and pushy,' he paused, 'beautiful but bloody dangerous if you don't know what you're doing.'

This conversation went on for weeks. I was rushing all over the south of England looking at property. There was something wrong with each one – too small, too big, not enough land, too much land, too modern, too near neighbours – and then I found it – Broadhurst Manor. An old, sixteenth-century manor house, set in green and leafy Sussex, it had eight stables and barns. It also had four lakes, two woodlands and was everything I could ever have wanted.

I actually went to see the house after an invitation by the owner on a cold and frosty unwelcoming day in October. And apart from sheep nibbling in the fields, there seemed to be nothing around. The manor house stood splendid and ancient behind two enormous, wrought-iron gates; its timber front and enormously tall chimneys were reminiscent of old oil paintings where farmers leaned on carts and white-aproned maids tottered around the garden carrying wooden buckets. Leading away from the house was a straight path to two more wrought-iron gates and into an old stone yard with a natural pond in the middle. At the back of this house everything suddenly turned to stone. There was no wood, just large stones laid upon each other like an old church, with great, patterned, oak doors, wide windows and leaden pipes with little carved squares at the top, a sunken garden and just one squirrel leaping about among the oak trees.

I told my sons Carl and Nigel about this house. It couldn't have been a worse day – rain and sleet and wind. But the moment they saw the big iron gates, they smiled their young smiles and made plans for my life in Broadhurst Manor. Leaving Zoffany House was hard. I had loved it so much. I thought about the river and the ducks and geese that gathered round my gate each day and the swans slowly shifting, sharing the bread I threw. My upbringing in a city like Liverpool only remained in my accent. Now my heart and mind were seeking all things natural, all things free.

I already knew a man called Peter, who ran a rescue centre. I had been to see it often and now I heard that the old lady who owned it had died and that it was possibly going to close down. I was telling Peter about my new home and each sentence seemed to draw me nearer to realising that it was the perfect place for a sanctuary. It fills me with alarm when I remember that I said to him, without properly knowing him, 'Why don't you come and bring all your animals? You can live in the cottage. We will run a sanctuary.'

The immediate thing to have done would have been to have built various avaries and special shelters for the variety of animals that Peter was bringing with him.

I remember lying in my bed the night before I left Zoffany, watching the moon pass behind the old oak tree in the next garden. I thought of my own madness at taking dogs, cats, hundreds of birds, tortoises, fish and Bell to this place.

'You're crazy,' said a voice, said my friends, said everybody. That is everybody except Marna and Len. They did not always understand me but always took the view that we must be whom we are, and when I asked them to come with me the answer was 'Yes'. They, too, had cats and dogs so it would be a better place for their animals and we would then wait and see what was in store for all of us.

The whole of Chiswick must have been astounded by the spectacle of our move from Zoffany to Broadhurst: two vans, one for furniture and one for animals. I sat on the tailpiece of one of the vans, finding various places for various creatures. Bell was the only one free; he sat on my shoulder preening himself. Unfazed by the commotion, Sieva, the rabbit, had a cabbage leaf hanging out of his mouth. The birds were a bit fidgety, but two of them began to sing as if nothing was happening. The rest, a little frightened, fluffed up their feathers and took refuge in their little boxes. The two tortoises and two guinea pigs travelled together in an old cardboard box, and the large fish basked in a baby bath with wire over the top. Egor and the cats sat together at the back of the van on blankets, totally unmoved by the whole thing. Marna and Len travelled in their own car with their animals. As we drove off, I thought that it was possible that the residents around Zoffany House must have felt relieved at the departure of the resident loony.

It is difficult to explain what the journey was like. The actual movement and the mood of the animals were perfect, but it was full of 'What am I doing? How am I going to cope? Am I sure about all this?'

Tinged with dread, I thought, 'Oh God, this is my destiny, stand or fall, it is what I was meant to do – a sanctuary of my own.' Then my brain turned to things more financial – I tried to battle against this too. 'Writing isn't anything,' I thought. 'Fame is only fleeting. It's no fun finding pictures of yourself in the papers, growing angry because you're growing older. No more deadlines, worries about the right words on the page, meetings with heads of departments.' I could hear 'His' voice in my head: 'You're mad, darling.' I had dreamed of us both running naked in the woodlands, swimming in the lakes – I was past forty but I didn't look it, I certainly didn't think like it. But he had grown into that terrible word 'sensible'. He conducted his life like he would an orchestra; up and down with the mood of the music, coming in and out of shadows and learning each time the light came.

Some hours later, we joined Peter with his fourteen vehicles, containing all the creatures from the sanctuary. Trucks, vans, Range Rovers, trailers, horseboxes and a variety of animal noises assaulted the peace and tranquillity of the little Sussex village in Horsted Keynes. The geese, which hadn't stopped complaining since the beginning of the journey, were poking their agitated beaks through the slats as we turned into Broadhurst Manor's drive. Soon we entered the main yard with its stables, sheds, a sand school and nearby paddocks. It was nearly evening and with all our other friends who helped us with this journey, we set about placing various animals in various stables and sheds, putting water and food in, separating the agitators, making special beds for the young, stabling ten horses, rounding up fifty chickens and getting them to go into a unit – all this took till gone midnight. At the end of it all, we succumbed to total exhaustion and one by one slid down by the side of the stables and fell asleep sitting up in the yard.

Our cockerels heralded the dawn from inside one of the trucks and stiff and pained, we started the almost impossible task of accommodating each group of animals with a place suitable for their temperament and their needs. No goats with horses, yet. No chickens with geese, yet. Certainly not the so-called tame fox with anything edible. All but the injured and sick pigeons were put in a temporary large aviary – others were housed in a large building which was heated and would eventually become our hospital room. In between all of this, of course, devoted friends were running in and out of Broadhurst making tea and coffee and keeping us alive.

It is hard to describe the total disorder of our arrival. We didn't have neighbours as such but the cottages that were closest to us, perhaps a quarter of a mile away, would surely have heard the noise. The man who saw and heard most was the one time owner of Broadhurst Manor, indeed he was born there. We had to trundle past his house in the early morning and I'm sure that moment often returns to him in the form of a nightmare.

Now and then, I consoled my tired self by seeing a picture of me, sitting on the old wall by the lake writing wonderful scripts. I thought I had escaped from all that but the truth is I never will escape from my pen. However, Peter, who was knowledgeable about all creatures having run a sanctuary for years, seemed to know everything that was needed by these animals, and I left him to sort out the sanctuary while I went to the house to assist Carl and Nigel who had unpacked my furniture, placed it in various rooms and more or less made the house comfortable.

I knew there were lots of rooms, forty odd and I knew there were at least twelve bathrooms. This is because Broadhurst Manor had once been used as a retreat for drug addicts. Fortunately, apart from the odd, awful, modern bathroom which had been built, the really old part of the house was intact. Several days later, with everything almost in order, Carl and Nigel fled back to their life in Liverpool. There was just me, Marna and Len, gazing at each other vacantly across an enormous oak table wondering 'What next?'

What actually happened next was that we were burgled. While we slept, during the third week of being there, someone broke into what we called the Big Room. All my silver was taken and my favourite collection of clocks. There was only thing that slightly comforted me – we had not yet entirely unpacked and I still had some beloved treasures in boxes in the cellar.

Each room had a name. There was the Green Room, the Herb Room, the Feast Room, the Pink Room, the Big Room, St George's Room, the Lake Room and so it went on. At the end of the one-hundred-foot hall, I noticed a door, which I believed was a big cupboard. My sons had opened it and it led into four other big rooms. The sheer excitement of this amazing house stopped me from thinking how foolish I was to leap into a situation of this enormity so quickly, and how disastrous it could possibly become.

A walk round the lakes took away that thought and already our ducks and geese were on the water, preening and calling as if they had always been there. A heron flew above me and when I looked up, to my horror, it had a tiny baby chick of some kind in its beak. Its little legs were wriggling and it settled on a partly submerged tree in my lake and proceeded to swallow this poor live thing. Although I had always loved the idea of the countryside, this incident taught me right away that there were some things I was not going to like about it.

In the evenings, caught in the lights that come and go at the back of the house, were so many wild creatures – badgers, foxes, rabbits, pheasants and all kinds of others that I did not recognise. The idea of the fox worried me – surely he would eat all the others, so immediately I set up a plan whereby every night we were to put out a load of food for the fox. I was lucky enough to get lots of bags of slightly-past-their-sell-by-date dog biscuits from a local shop – this made up most of the banquet for the fox. And to this day, the fox, or should I now say foxes, who queue up for this feast every night, have never touched a single animal of ours. There was so much more to discover; blossoming trees, grassy hills, slopes down to the lake with the footmarks of many creatures, steps twisting and turning that seemed to go nowhere, enormous, ancient oak trees, hundreds of years old, five of which stood together on a leaf-covered slope. I found myself touching them and talking to them – they were so ancient, so wise. There was a grassy pathway that led all round the four lakes. It curved upwards in a way that you would not notice and suddenly, when you reached the fourth lake, you were looking down at it through trees, daffodils or bluebells. I knew that this place was going to be my final move – the place where I would live, learn and, one day, die.

Of course dressing up was out of the question. Gone now were the high heels, the swirling silk skirts, Victorian blouses, the long, amber, onyx beads – in fact, gone now was all the glamour. It was jeans and wellies and funny hats and hands brown and worn.

I had talked to 'Him' about this place, of course, but was so busy and exhausted during the actual move that all that passed between us was a few phone calls, hurried and filled with 'I'll see you soon'. One day, I was standing in plenty of mud in my green wellies, feeding the fish in my lake, when 'He' suddenly appeared – it was like a big film. I ran towards him, or should I say, I squelched towards him. This was so romantic – he actually put out his arms.

'Oh God,' he said.

'What? What?'

'It's beautiful.'

'I told you.'

I took him by the sleeve and towed him into the house, and in and out of every room. He ran his hands down the dark slats of oak, the heavy oak doors, he touched the wide oak floors and he opened and shut the heavy curtains, thrust his head through open windows, tried to read what was carved on the six-hundred-year-old fire back, rang the gate bell and then he looked at me and said, smiling, 'You are . . .'

'Mad, I know, I know.'

That was the first night he spent at Broadhurst Manor. We walked to his car the following morning and he ruffled my hair. He was not a man of presents and boxes of chocolates. When he bought me flowers, he would leave them in a milk bottle in the sink – perhaps it was because he had witnessed so many actors and actresses receiving such enormous bouquets and he wanted to be more original.

Chapter 24

LINDA, LINDA

By now, Linda McCartney and I were close friends. She often rang and asked me to go and see her and we spent hours trying to put this cruel world to rights. She and Paul often had get-togethers in London and during this time, I met lots of other people, not necessarily television people, but well-known, well-revered people. And as Linda was intolerant of those who didn't concern themselves with the plight of animals, most of them could be described as animal carers. One of the things I loved about Linda was her ability to be unafraid of her feelings. She was especially emotional about animals, but her views about all things she would make known openly and passionately. Linda was adamant that people should not eat meat. She was totally unafraid of saying so and would spend much time trying to make the so-called 'meat eaters' understand the cruelty of the slaughterhouse.

We spent long sunny days at her home in Rye, drinking tea and talking. Linda was so passionate, so strong. I recall the time a lady stopped me and said, 'Will you tell Linda her veggie sausages are too greasy.' I did this when we next met. Linda said immediately, 'Hang on, Carla.'

Then I heard her on a nearby phone in her kitchen.

'Hi,' she said, 'Linda here. Look, it's about the sausages. I want them off the shelves.' (Pause) 'No, no, now.' (Longer pause). 'No, not tomorrow, I said now.' (Yet another pause). 'Yeah, I'll talk about it later. Yeah, yeah, every one now.'

She put the phone down and turning to me said, 'OK, that's done, let's go and see the horses.'

Linda's grey-and-black Appaloosa horse was beautiful. She loved him with all her heart. She got effortlessly onto his back and took him off for a gallop, not like me. My sanctuary had already introduced me to the perils of horses. Their sheer size and intelligence had always bothered me. One raise of the head and you could be catapulted into the nearest tree. Years ago, in Spain, I tried riding and was treated to a totally unrequested tour of the Spanish countryside on the back of an old, sore, stricken horse, which I soon realised was trying to get away from the situation he was in, being ridden every day in the hot sunshine, riddled with saddle sores. The next day, I remember, I bought some antiseptic cream, went back to the riding school and treated all his sores with it. I did this every day, twice a day, during that holiday and Eric, who was with me then, helped me to choose a cushion to put underneath the saddle.

Linda and I had plans for the future. Her cookery book had already come out and was received enthusiastically. 'OK,' she said, 'let's do another. I'll do the cooking, you do the talking.' Sadly, it didn't happen. One day, as we sat in her kitchen, she told me, 'Look, I don't want to go on about this, but I have this problem – cancer they call it.' My heart plunged and before I could speak, she said, 'Let's go and see Sparky.' Sparky being the parrot which lived in a large aviary in her gardens. She was out of the door before I could respond. Neither of us ever discussed her illness again. I knew quite definitely that Linda did not want to talk about it. She knew that I knew and that was it and I upheld her wish. We played about with her camera, arranging flowers in vases, arranging large melons in groups, taking pictures of our dogs, of each other and the strange ritual of silence remained.

I was still struggling to reintroduce myself as a scriptwriter, but the change in the BBC hampered me. Slowly but surely, I was becoming a country girl. One part of me wanted to be just that, but there was still that other half which crowded my head – thoughts, ideas – I couldn't rid myself of them without a pen in my hand. It was becoming harder not to write. I learned to go between the house and the sanctuary. By now, I had employed other people to work in the house and in the garden and several to run the sanctuary. All this was costing me lots of money and I wasn't earning any. Candi, who did all the office work for the sanctuary and for the house, worked closely with Leonard, who had now become my book keeper. Between them, they shielded me from the business side of things, which is an area that I could never ever manage.

During this particular time, I got to know Rory Clarke, a farmer whose house was the nearest to mine and who owned the nine hundred acres of land surrounding me. He also once owned Broadhurst Manor and indeed was born there. I am told, that in all the pubs the conversation was, 'Guess who's moved into the Manor House – bloody Carla Lane.' Rory reared sheep on his land. He reared and treated them excellently, although he did have a gamekeeper who seemed to love killing things most of all. One day, I saw this young man stop his car, shoot a crow and drive on leaving it bouncing in the grass with pain. By the time I had climbed the fence and got to it, it was dead. I went to see Rory and found him to be a very kind man, indeed, a gentleman, and I have never been able to understand why such a man was involved so much in all the things I hated – hunting, shooting, snaring and letting out his land to people who did the same and more. However, we always managed to discuss our views in a sensible way, and he has brought me nearer to understanding that the people who indulge in these things are as passionate about them as I am against them.

Peter was running the sanctuary well. He had a charming nature and attracted a lot of volunteers. Most of the animals – indeed, almost all of them – came to us suffering from injury or illness. Peter dealt with these very professionally and as the sanctuary grew more serious cases began to arrive, and our wildlife guide book was the only thing to guide us. Now we had to order everything a hospital room needed so that we could attend to all these creatures. Simple things such as bandages, plasters, special foods and more complicated things like painkillers, antibiotics.

There came a time when I did not always approve of what Peter was doing and after a while, I spoke to him about it. A terrible rift grew between us. I kept coming across things that I had never thought about. Sometimes, I realised you could get staff who were very good at looking after the animals, but who could not get in on time or took a lot of time off. Then you could have people who turned up at the right time and never took any time off, but didn't actually grasp how animals should be cared for. There were other people who were brilliant with the animals and always kept good time, but their confidence would surge to the extent that they were making decisions without you knowing and some of them were wrong, and this describes Peter. Finally the gap between us urged him to leave.

There was one, however, to whom none of this applied. Her name was Lorraine. She was a qualified veterinary nurse and applied for a job. She came from my home city of Liverpool and she had that lovely soft Liverpool accent, a real deadpan sense of humour and above all was a brilliant nurse. I remember in particular how one day a pigeon was brought in which seemed to have injuries of every kind on every part of it. We stood together looking down at this heap of feathers and blood. Lorraine picked it up and held it in front of me.

'I can't do anything with this, can I?'

I didn't say anything, I just looked at her, and she said, 'Yes I can,' and we immediately went into the routine of Save the Bird. For two hours she bent over it, cleaning, disinfecting, administering this and that and doing loads and loads of stitching. He looked very much like a little patchwork quilt. He was gaping and unable to stand. Gently, she placed him in a heated cage and she said to me, 'We'll have to wait and see now, won't we?' And in the morning, there he was – there was no other way of describing it – he looked a mess, but he was breathing soundly. He had stopped gaping and was showing signs of wanting his breakfast. And so this bird began his journey back to freedom.

Sadly, Lorraine had to leave. She wanted to learn more about many things and needed to go elsewhere to do that. I will never forget seeing her sitting in the little cottage that belonged to Broadhurst, watching television, eating something vegetarian, with a chicken on her shoulder, another chicken in a basket on the back of her settee, a sick cat lying by the heater on a soft pillow, two geese in the kitchen with two babies, one not well, a one-legged pigeon perched on the television table and her other two cats sprawled on the settee along with her two dogs, one of them with a chicken resting on its back. Lorraine has gone on to learn so much more and apart from the people I have now she is the one I treasured most.

But life presents us with as many prizes as problems. A phone call came and a voice said, 'I am a retired veterinary man and I am bored. I would like very much to come to your sanctuary and help.' We were elated. Of course, we thought it might be someone undesirable, but along came Brian – Dr Brian Alps – a man over fifty, quiet, gentle and bursting with knowledge and experience. We could not believe that he could possibly be interested in our sanctuary, but he was. He came with his large leather case and his precious instruments arrayed in it and he took the simple broken wing and mended it and the almost totally crushed animal and put it back together. The seriously ill, the 'don't know what it is', were reasons to consult Brian. By now we had equipped our tiny operating theatre with all the things he required. One of the staff learned to assist him and in that little room he performed magical things. Animals, which would have surely died without him and often looked as though they might, would be found the following morning, perky, bright eyed, demanding food and water. Brian never gave up; sometimes, he would spend hours putting a mutilated pigeon back together. There wasn't a single animal that he didn't know and understand, and it was he who turned our sanctuary into something much more, a place where animals didn't come to die but to be given the finest chance of life.

It wasn't long before my writing mania reappeared. This time, I was suddenly into writing a song. I called it 'The Other Children of the World'. A friend called Alan, a brilliant musician, played and sang this song, which was recorded on a CD, but I have never known quite what to do with it.

I called the sanctuary Animaline and I began to write articles and for a while I was content to do this, and the money I received kept us solvent.

We had begun to publish a newsletter for the sanctuary and this tempted people to send us donations, Animaline was now becoming well known. In an effort to keep the funds moving, I decided to rent a shop and called it The Carla Lane Animal shop. This, too, brought us a bit of money but not much for the first year, after which I found a manageress, called Ann, who had the time to devote to it and to this day it is helping Animaline out of the financial morass it keeps falling into. For a while money for repeats of my programmes on television kept things going, but because of the complete change in comedy, these did not suffice and I had already started to dip very deeply into money I had miraculously saved.

'He' was getting fed up. Snatched moments together were not what he wanted. When I went to stay in his flat in London, I was frustrated because of my worries about what was happening at Broadhurst and when he came to stay at the manor it was not unusual for me to have to abandon him in order to help in the hospital room or muck out a herd of animals. This resulted in him creeping around the kitchen, opening drawers, gazing into the fridge, trying to find something that his stomach could accommodate. I never liked cooking, and had forgotten any rudimentary culinary skills I might once have had. The potatoes were burnt, the peas clung to each other in terror, the gravy dropped onto the plate and coagulated immediately, the custard outwitted the jelly and landed like a stone in the dish – everything was either undercooked, overcooked, or badly cooked, and by the time I came back to the house, he was too weak to be remotely romantic.

Another problem had arisen. Egor had taken to sleeping on my bed. This new life had unsettled him and because he kept getting told off for chasing the animals he became all wimpy and wanted to be with me, in my car, on my rounds and on my bed. There was really not enough room for anyone else. Any passion we attempted was interrupted by the mournful sounds of Egor moving about at the bottom of the bed and protesting about the intrusion and different sounds altogether as he landed on the floor, having been kicked off the bed. Egor knew his rights and there was no way you could get him to stay on the floor.

'Lock him out,' said my tender lover.

'Lock him out, lock my dog out?'

Bearing in mind that greater love hath no woman, I did try locking Egor out. But Irish wolfhounds don't just scratch at the door, they annihilate it. Soon, the old doorknob was whizzing round and the door was open. Egor would leap onto the bed and 'He' would leap off the bed. Because we were naked at the time these scenes carried a more significant amount of embarrassment. He would leave; he would always leave. Whenever anything went wrong, the only thing he knew was to leave, forcing me to write a poem called 'Go Now'.

On this particular occasion, as we both dressed hurriedly and I followed him down the stairs and he was about to cross the yard, he was accosted by two agitated Canada geese who happened to be night walking. One had the leg of his trousers and the other a corner of the coat that he was carrying. He limped towards his car, towing the geese as he went, neither of them would let go and he was just as adamant – his goal was his car and his quick getaway. While he was in the process of trying to open his car door, I arrived. I eventually managed to coax their beaks open and send them off in a different direction. He was inspecting the large tear in his coat.

'You're not very clever with geese are you, and soon you'll run out of coats.'

He nearly smiled.

'I'm sorry,' I said. 'This place is not right for you, I am not right for you. I'm sorry.' This tiny soliloquy had some effect on him. Instead of slamming the door and driving off, he stopped and with a look of 'Oh shit, what should I do – go or stay?' he got out of his car. We went back to the house. Our passion was punctuated by the sound of mating pigeons on the windowsill of the bedroom.

'Is there anywhere we can go that is not dominated by animals?' he said.

'No,' I said.

Chapter 25

SOLACE

It was strange not having scripts to write, not having rehearsals, meetings and the excitement of seeing a programme made. The BBC as I knew it had vanished. I was called in once to talk to the new Head of Comedy but I left her office knowing that she had no room or time for my kind of comedy. It was all for the young now, the new cult of free love, say what you like, be outrageous but youth had shaken hands and parted from me some time before. I still had enough money to stave off poverty and got into the habit of walking Egor, messing about in the garden, gazing into my goldfish pond, going out in the evenings with friends, lots of dinners, lots of laughing, but without writing it seemed like lots of nothing.

A new extension of the BBC had been built further along Wood Lane. It's all black and grey and glass, but the old feeling of 'Wow, I'm in the BBC' had gone. Great shoals of young and loudly confident people flooded the stairways and the big entrance hall. Heads of departments are no longer the tested, slightly silver-haired gentlemen and women who had been weaned on BBC television and who were acquainted with the needs of a very mixed English audience. People who liked best of all to see themselves, either in comedy or drama. Of course, one has to go forwards with the new tide, but for me the new script requirements were not how I felt and feeling is the main ingredient in any work, so I found myself drifting in and out of my writing – half finishing things, abandoning things, having new thoughts – trying desperately to find something which fitted in with the new era. After several meetings with the Head of Comedy and long conversations about what she needed, I finally accepted that it was time to reinvent myself. I started off with a book of tortured poetry called *Dreams and Other Aggravations*. Instead of sending it to a publisher, some friends of mine published it privately so that the money could go to my sanctuary. It has brought and still is bringing in quite a lot of money.

I wrote a fifteen-minute story for radio about a middle-aged lady who was having a secret liaison with her gardener. It was all about her anxiety, her guilt and her worry about what might happen to her safe and uneventful marriage. The gardener was killed by a car as he was crossing the road outside her house on the way to visit her. She hears about it in the post office, and without going too much and too boringly into the story, she rushes back to her marriage and decides to live with the yawning gap of loneliness, filled only by the memories of drinking coffee in her little paved back yard with the gardener.

This barren part of my career went hand in hand with 'His' life, too. Young and lively presenters were all over the BBC with their ideas and reformation. They outnumbered the existing staff, like the sparrows used to outnumber all other birds. So there we were, in our early forties and heading towards redundancy. During this time our relationship took another step, I would say sideways rather than forwards. We began sitting in the car in country lanes gazing at houses; old houses, big houses, half built houses. We were drifting back to a time before in Chiswick, knowing full well that it could never happen. Occasionally, those giddy days of ice skating and flirting and showing off, the time when I fell flat on my face in front of the man who was to be my husband, kept coming into my mind. Everything seemed so simple then; being in love, getting married, having babies, but the complications of 'Him' made me realise that it's not really all like that.

The only love that seemed to stay with me was the love of Liverpool. I longed to hear the tune of the Scouse accent. I missed the clanging sound of the bin men, the chap who used to knock on my door selling cups, saucers and plates – how in an effort to show that they were sound, he would clang them together and they would fall to pieces on the doorstep. But undeterred, with true Liverpool skulduggery, he would say 'Now then love, that is what 'appens with other people's crockery, but not mine'. He'd already be picking up another cup and waving it about. 'Mine are strong, they have no hidden cracks, love, nothing like that.' He did not bang the second lot together of course, but started wrapping them up in newspaper, making it impossible for you to refuse to buy them. I also had a longing to visit Quiggins, the antique shop, the town's market, to sit among dive-bombing seagulls and watch the dark brown River Mersey arguing with small boats, and men in caps leaving the ship-building yards carrying a parcel. They would tip their caps to the watchman. 'Tarra,' they would say and that one word would stop the watchman asking them what was in the parcel beneath their arm.

And just as I was near to giving up writing and going back to all those things, a break came. The BBC asked me to write a comedy for Jim Davidson. I had met him briefly but knew him well on television. A company called Deepwater, owned by my friend Maria, was going to produce it. I took up my pen and after gazing at it for a long time, wondering what it was for, I began to write. I called the series *The Cuckoo*. It was about a man who left his real love to marry the girl he got pregnant. It turned out to be a happy marriage and they now lived in a nice house in a nice road and everything was bliss. A beautiful lady moved in next door. It turned out to be his first love, the one he left. It was not a coincidence, that was important for the strength of the series, as she explained: 'I wanted to watch you, that's all; to see what I missed. Nothing more. I wanted you to see me, too.'

The man really tried not to fall in love with her again. He did everything to avoid her but his wife kept reminding him how awful it was that he should watch the lady next door struggling in the garden, trying to mend her coal shed, coping with all the things that an empty house provides, and he was torn between listening to his wife and wanting desperately to go next door but afraid of the consequences.

It was a good script. I felt that and Jim, in particular, loved it. He kept hugging me and telling me how wonderful it was going to be for him to do this different and exciting thing. Maria pulled out every stop to make it work. The atmosphere in the rehearsal room was on a high, the surroundings were beautiful, the food was of the finest and Jim and the cast learned and played their parts magnificently. I remember thinking, 'It's all coming back, all the excitement that writers experience when watching their work being performed'.

In those days, the BBC had a new idea and that was to call all the heads of departments together, to give new comedy programmes three days to rehearse and then present the programme and then, based on what the bosses saw and how they felt, a commission would either be given or not. Together with a selected team, Maria conducted the three-day rehearsal with absolute love for the script and those taking part in it and we presented the BBC hierarchy with what we considered to be a really good programme. Jim, who was a comedian, had now blossomed into an actor, a sad and funny actor. In a specially chosen room with an audience of VIPs and the smell of a pending lunch, we all watched this being played and I felt we couldn't lose. Indeed, everybody clapped for several minutes and people came rushing up to us saying how pleased they were. It was like the old days, I was back.

Three weeks later, Maria rang me to say that the BBC had turned it down. I was heartbroken. I took the blame. I told myself that perhaps it wasn't a good script, perhaps I had lost touch, perhaps the talent I had had made an escape – these were dark, dark days. Finally, I learned that a dispute between Jim Davidson and the BBC was the cause of this collapse. It was less hard to bear knowing that the script was not to blame, but everything that happened now seemed to be ringing the death knell of my career.

Sometime later, Jim Davidson did a two-hour concert for my animal sanctuary. There were thousands in the audience and he began by coming on stage and saying 'This is for Carla. I know you're out there somewhere, love, and it's for you and your animals'. He went on to give the funniest show I have ever seen and to make nearly £7000 for my sanctuary.

Chapter **26**

CASUALTIES

In the sanctuary, I found it hard to witness the plight of some of our inmates: the fox that was half strangled in a snare and had got free only to be hit by a car; the squirrel that had got himself caught up in some wire and was almost cut in half; the duck who peeped out of his pen and had his beak snapped off by a fox; the horse that was old and worn and Belsen thin; the deer standing in the middle of the road with some of his cheek hanging down like a piece of meat and one leg shattered. All these and many more lived to see another day.

The time came when I was able now to look after the hospital room, if necessary, by myself. My heart used to beat fast every time I saw the dreaded gates opening and somebody approaching with a box. I remember one person came holding a large white dove with blood streaming from its throat. I tried to stem the blood by holding a pad against the wound but it spilled onto the floor. I couldn't give him a painkiller or anything else until I had stopped it, so in desperation I unwound a whole roll of cotton wool and wrapped it round his neck time and time again. It didn't quite seep through so I knew I had won that one. I gave him a painkiller and an antibiotic and injected some saline to make up for the loss of blood. By this time, he was gaping badly and I was sure I had lost. I settled him down on a soft pillow and he became calm, his eyes were closed and that was not a good sign, so I was loathe to leave him and I put my head down on the operating table. A long time afterwards, I was awakened by a rustling sound, and there he was preening himself!

The land surrounding Broadhurst Manor was probably once farming land, where cattle and sheep and chickens and turkeys and all things wild grazed. Now this whole area seems devoted to hunting, shooting and killing, ridding these green carpets of grass of all living things. These included deer, rabbits, foxes, pigeons, magpies, crows and squirrels. I often stop my car and search the land in front of me and to the side of me for something that's moving. The only sign of life is the rabbit, and they suffer from myxomatosis and soon die. 'Why,' I keep asking, 'why?' Land management is the answer I usually get. The only things allowed to spend a measured lifetime there are those animals which will eventually be hunted or shot. I search with my binoculars often, sitting silently in my car, or looking through my highest window, waiting, watching for something to move.

Once, as I drove up the lane, I saw a stoat. He came from the pond in somebody's garden. I couldn't take my eyes off him – long, lean and mean, part of the fabric of our countryside and miraculously he was alive. I haven't seen his like since. If you ask a farmer why he shoots pigeons, jackdaws, magpies, rabbits or squirrels, he will tell you that they are vermin. It seems to me that the word 'vermin' is a term used for any creature that outwits man – the fox does this best. But how hard it is for him. He needs food; he can't hunt for it because he is hunted, he can't go out at night and find it because of the lampers, who shine a long distance torch into his eyes, mesmerising him and then shooting him. At one point, even if he caught something, he couldn't take it back to his den because he was either dug out by man or by hounds. The process of getting to grips with a chicken is not easy, either; with both wings flapping, it is hard to get control of it. Sometimes, the fox gets control of one wing but the flapping of the other makes it impossible for him to run off with it. It is then that he drops that one and tries another and the only time he can leave the chicken pen is when he has got both wings under control. People say that he deliberately wounds chickens but the wounds are caused by the need to be able to hold on to his meal.

Other sad occasions occur when the larger animals, such as deer, badgers and foxes, arrive at the sanctuary. Deer have a quiet, seemingly calm, manner of dealing with an injury. It is misleading, as they are often seriously hurt in a way that is not evident. The badger is less subtle. He is only quiet when he is badly hurt. Anything less than that and you are in danger of losing of an arm or a leg.

The saddest of all cases, for me, is the myxomatosis-infested rabbit. It is a dirty, smelly, cruel disease designed by man. As it progresses, the eyes are filled with pus and lose their sight; the entire body is under attack, a slow erosion takes place, the rabbit is almost decomposing and he can go on like this for some time. One extraordinary thing is that a rabbit in this situation will often eat a whole apple, wash his face and preen his body, then very carefully settle down to die, as if he had planned it all.

I now want to tell you the story of a fish. I choose to do this because most people cannot imagine there ever being an interesting story about a fish!

One day, the gardener came in and said that the heron had visited my pond. Two fish were dead; one was still alive. I arrived just in time to see another of my staff raising a stone above another fish that was not quite dead.

'Don't. Don't!' I yelled.

The man looked at me in amazement.

'He's half dead,' he said.

'Leave him to me, if you don't mind,' I said.

He went away, muttering things about stupid women.

The fish was a bright red, gold colour. He was twelve inches long and had a wound at the nape of his neck where the heron's sharp beak had struck, but he was still breathing, and so I took him into the house and placed him in the kitchen in a bucket half filled with water and a tap dripping into it for oxygen. I called this fish 'Tear'. I gave him some antibiotic liquid and he took it from a spoon and I covered his wound with a thing called Introsite, which would keep it free of germs. After a couple of days in the bucket, Tear, although he was almost lifeless, was still with us, so I moved him to a large bath in a bright, sunlit bathroom with plants all around. He just lay at the bottom of the water for two days. The beak of the heron had touched his spine and this meant that it was impossible for him to move. The only thing I didn't know was: for how long, or would it be forever?

I gently held him each morning and floated him on my hand. After several days, little parts of his side fins began to move and after a minute of this, he was tired. I decided to build him an underwater rest bed out of soft cloth and each time I exercised him, I put him back on this. As you can imagine, I did not get any support from anyone – they all thought I was mad, but each time I went to Tear, he tried to move his fins a little more. Sometimes, he achieved this; other times, he could not move them at all. There were moments when I thought, 'You can't go on like this,' and then I would look at those coal-black eyes, which seemed to say, 'I am trying'.

Within three weeks, Tear was showing excitement each time I entered the bathroom. His under fins would move considerably when I called his name and when I floated some food in front of him he was able to take it in immediately. One day, I went into the bathroom and Tear was nowhere to be seen. I panicked. 'He's jumped out,' I thought. But no – he was resting among all the plants at the end of the bath, the significant thing being that he must have travelled some distance to get there.

I bought two other smaller fish to keep him company. They soon befriended him and spent most of their time hovering above him. They did not seem to mind the fact that he did not move. One day, when I entered the bathroom and called his name, Tear rose very quickly to the top of the water, did a couple of pas-de-deux and sank again. I was elated. 'I have won,' I thought, 'you are going to make it.' From that day on, he made steady progress, but there was no movement of his major back fins, the ones which in the end would propel him properly and steer him. I waited for two months and our relationship was limited by his limitations. Four times a day, I would go and call him; four times he would come to the end of the bath with his little friends above him, but finally he would sink to the bottom and I had to put him back on his rest and there he would stay until my next visit.

I realised all along that he would probably never be the big, gallant hero that he should have been. There were many of his offspring now thriving in my pond and I grew upset every time I thought of all the things that were due to him but that he was denied. Sometimes, these little trips along the bath towards me seemed enough, but only for him. They made me see only his limitations and I made up my mind to end it all, but it was impossible. He would either do some other little thing that he had never done before, or those eyes would come towards me through the water.

One day, fate took it out of my hands. He developed fin rot – this is something which fish often suffer and, with treatment, can easily discard, but with Tear there was no help from his damaged immune system and it began to spread. Finally, setting aside all emotions, closing my mind to everything but the fact that here was a fish that would never be a fish, I had him put to sleep painlessly by my veterinary nurse and I buried him in the garden surrounding the pond where he had spent seven joyful years.

I felt I had to tell this story because I learned from it that fish have feelings just like any creature which has a beating heart. He may have been frustrated, he may have been deeply unhappy, but what I shall always remember is his joyful greeting each time I walked into the bathroom and the way he tried so hard to get better, but the heron had dealt him a limiting blow. I shall never forget Tear.

Chapter **27**

SOME KIND OF WAR

Live exports were back! I immediately phoned my very dear friend and confidante, the Colonel. 'What can I do?' I said, 'What can I do?'

'What you always do Carla, just yell.'

At this time, as many as fifteen trucks left every day from Shoreham. I couldn't help but believe that this was fate because Broadhurst Manor was quite close to Shoreham, so it was virtually on my doorstep. Almost immediately, hundreds, and probably thousands, of people were alerted and on the first morning of the trucks leaving Shoreham, they gathered and I was one of them. We were surrounded by police, who were quite calm, and indeed we laughed and joked with them. We knew when the trucks were close because the traffic was diverted and suddenly everything went quiet, very quiet, as the laughing and joking stopped. We lined the streets of Shoreham with police flanked behind us. One of our members had a drum and as soon as the yellow coats of the approaching police (who were surrounding the trucks) were seen as far back as Brighton, he began a slow beat on the drum. We moved forwards to meet them – it was a long, slow, heart-racing, few minutes. As for myself, I didn't know what I was going to do when we met up with them. Was I going to lie on the floor, or do something stupid like cling to a truck? Was I going to run away, even, once the real panic began? In fact, moments before the actual trucks caught up with us, the huge yellow blob of policemen ran towards us and scattered us. But we were prepared and very soon we were running alongside the dilapidated trucks, trying to touch the faces of the animals. The young calves and lambs, some were covered with excrement from the animals in the tiers above them, and the slats were so wide that they could put their whole head and face through them – such a pitiful sight. Some were obviously ill; others too young to travel this way. Others could be seen disappearing, obviously falling to the floor and probably being trodden on by the rest. We followed the trucks all the way to the docks, where they stopped and waited, I imagine, to be told when they could go on board.

By now thousands of people had gathered. We were like little insects crawling all over the trucks, wherever we could get – underneath them, on top of them and police were crawling after us, grabbing our clothes, our hair, anything they could. It is hard for me to describe the emotion and anger these gatherings created. It was a cold winter and it wasn't easy waiting for so long for the first sight of the trucks. By the time they did arrive, we were racked with anger. We thought of the politicians, sitting in their comfortable leather seats of the House of Commons, deciding that this should happen and one lost faith in the people who governed us. It seems there wasn't one of them against this cruellest of all cruel trades.

But I was wrong.

I had written a letter to each and every one of the MPs and out of the one hundred and sixty letters sent, I received one hundred and fifty-four agreeing that this was an unforgivably cruel trade – indeed, I was invited to have a meeting with these MPs. But I had already had meetings with all kinds of political people – I had sent letters to the Prime Minister and all the people who had anything to do with the laws of this trade – and nothing ever came of it. So it seemed more important to go every morning at ten o'clock to Shoreham.

For some reason – possibly because I was the only one with a loud hailer – I seemed to have become a leader. By leader, I don't mean I was any braver or better than the rest, but I was able to converse with the police and because of my loud hailer, also to converse with the people.

139

Eventually, the kind of relationship I had with the police was one where they would say to me 'OK, Carla, if you make them promise not to do anything unacceptable, we will allow them to block the road for a few minutes', or 'OK, Carla, if they promise to stay on the pavement when the trucks come, we will let them go down the slipway'. But it was always absolute mayhem. Emotions always seized us and it was nothing to be picked up by the scruff of the neck and chucked over the nearest hedge. Anyone going too near the truck was roughly handled and dragged away.

I will never forget the amazing cleverness of the protestors as a whole. So many brilliant, devious things were thought out to trick the police and to get near to the animals. The idea of getting near to them was not that we could do anything for them, but that we could perhaps touch them and promise them that the fight for all the rest of their kind would never end. As time passed, we became cleverer and cleverer. The police always seemed to have a hidden affection for us – one could see that many of them believed in what we were fighting for but all of them remained policemen after all and did their duty, which often caused us broken limbs, strained backs, black eyes and – even more painful – anger.

Sometimes, there was a hold up and we could walk along, touch, talk to, or give messages to the little faces peering through the slats. I will never forget the characters in Shoreham – so many of them. There was the little old lady who was delivered each morning by her daughter in the car. She was positioned behind a sort of Zimmer frame. A placard on a pole was attached to this Zimmer frame which read: 'Stop this cruel trade.' After a few days the message changed to 'We will stop this, we will stop this'. As frustration grew, so did the message, which finally read: 'Here we come you bastards.' There was a very posh lady who had a Union Jack printed on her sweater. She always carried her handbag and she would wave it about shouting to the drivers of the lorries, 'My husband is something big in the Water Board'. We were never sure what this was meant to do. Even the police smiled when they heard it. There were also many who tried to push the trucks back with their bare hands. This was something we all indulged in at least once, but you never did it a second time. And there was a man who had made a loud hailer out of a plastic traffic cone. His message was: 'Hang the exporters by the bollocks.' He had a tinny radio which he set on the sea wall playing very sombre music.

One day, we had been told not to step off the pavement and I accidentally did just that. A nearby policeman grabbed me, 'You're under arrest,' he said.

'What for?' I asked.

'You were told to stay on the pavement.'

He started pushing me around. Another policeman came along. I didn't struggle. I did as I was told. I got into the van and the door was slammed shut. Apparently, back at the scene of my arrest, the man who had been standing next to me when it happened said to the policeman who did it, 'I bet you don't know who that is.'

'I don't care who it is,' he responded.

'It's Carla Lane.'

'Oh fuck,' he said.

I was taken in this van to a rather dark place by the docks. I had to stand with the inevitable card in front of me and have my front and profile photograph taken. I was then hustled into a bigger van, which consisted of a small aisle along the middle and steel cages either side, each one occupied by a protestor. I was told to get into a cage, but because I am claustrophobic I pleaded that I should be able to stand in the passageway. It took a long time for the policeman, who had to go and see the driver before it was decided that I was to sit in the cage but with the door open and have a policeman guarding me. That I agreed to. I remember I was aching all over. I had used muscles that I had never used before even in my sanctuary, and because the local police station was full, we were now being taken to another station twelve miles away. When we arrived we were each placed in a cell. By this time we were hungry, very hungry.

'I can't do anything,' said one of the policeman. 'We don't have any food here – we're only a temporary police station.'

We all banged on our little wire panels pleading for a cup of tea or a cup of coffee. Finally, this poor policeman brought a tray with lots of cups of tea on it but they all had milk in them and all I could hear as he lifted each wire flap was 'Sorry mate, I'm a vegan, don't take milk', 'Sorry mate, no milk for me'.

And so it went on and even I said, 'No thank you, I don't drink milk.'

The poor man, totally frustrated, stood outside and shouted, 'Where do you think you are, the bloody Ritz?'

Outside the building there was a huge noise. Hundreds of protestors had fled to their cars and followed the van to the station. I was called into the office of the Chief Inspector and through the top half of the window opposite me, the bottom being boarded up, I could see flags, banners, cards, hands, people's faces appearing and disappearing as they jumped up, shouting 'We want Carla, we want Carla' and a few sentences perhaps I ought not to repeat. On the Chief Inspector's desk there was my beloved loud hailer, a ring and a bracelet and a watch, and he pointed to them and said, 'Are these yours?'

'Yes,' I said.

'Do you know why you're here Miss Lane?'

'Yes,' I said, 'I'm against cruelty to animals.'

'You are aware that this is a legal trade?'

'Yes I am.'

'Are you the ring leader?' he asked.

'No,' I said, 'I'm the only one with a proper loud hailer. We work together. This is a horrendous cruel trade. We want an end to it.'

He looked at me and there was a slight smile.

'Well you won't get it this way, Miss Lane.'

He had no need to tell me that. Greed and money, the need of farmers, the mindlessness of the politicians would see to that.

A like-minded man was Spike Milligan. He and I stood together in the pouring rain when the trucks were going through to the ships. We shouted and screamed together and the press surrounded us. As usual, he was funny and they could hardly concentrate on the photographs for his witty remarks. Later, at a party at Linda and Paul McCartney's house, we met again. There was a great crowd of well-known people there. When Spike needed to go to the bar, he would say 'Follow me', and he would tap his walking stick on the floor shouting, 'Aids, Aids, Aids here'. In spite of the fact that we all knew each other very well, everybody responded and drew back to let us through. He turned to me and said, 'It always works.' The last time I spoke to Spike was a few months before his death. He rang me. 'Carla,' he said, 'I want to send you some money for the sanctuary. Who do I make the cheque out to?'

'Animaline,' I told him.

'So I make cheques out to Animaline then?'

'Yes,' I said again. 'Thank you, thank you, Spike.'

'Animaline, you said.'

'Yes,' I said.

A few days later, a cheque came to me signed by him made out to 'The Adventurers'. I phoned to tell him this and Sheila, his wife, answered. 'He's always doing this,' she said.

As soon as I arrived home from the police station, I phoned 'Him'.

'Hello,' I said, 'it's me.'

'What are you doing for God's sake?'

'I've been . . .'

'Arrested, I know. It's all over the radio, in the evening papers.' Then his voice quietened. 'Darling, you'll never stop this, you'll get hurt.'

At this point I realised that he would never understand or ever have an affinity with animals, not because he was a cruel man – indeed, he was a kind man – but he was a disciplined man, a law-abiding man. I put the phone down – another little episode between 'Him' and me. I would have to sit quietly and reassess 'Him'. If all the rest of him was right for me that tiny piece of him that was so law abiding and righteous could not be ruled out because he patted dogs, stroked cats and watched wild birds.

In spite of his warning, I marched on. I decided to face all the people behind the live export trade. I started with DEFRA. I had had an invitation to one of their meetings. There, I unleashed my anger. I reminded them that my contemporaries and I had warned them of the possibility of disease because of overcrowding and general treatment of the animals and that we were right. They were very pleasant, but one could see apathy in their faces and in their eyes. They were caught in the stronghold of rules and regulations and all the other nonsense of European Union law. Every day after this, I found myself banging my fist on long, green baize tables. The terrifying sound in my voice almost frightened me, never mind them. No one was too important for my onslaught and after screaming my way through various government officials, unaccountably, I was invited by John Major, the then Prime Minister, to 10 Downing Street, and there among the gold-painted furniture and sombre portraits, I unleashed my anger yet again. Ten minutes into the meeting urgent news came for him. He had to leave and go to some other country for some problem. There was a great deal of coming and going throughout the house and, finally, I was given the company of someone else – I can't remember his name but he seemed important and close to the Prime Minister. My wrath continued. I made dramatic statements – I'm quite good at 'dramatic statements' concerning the cruelty of live exports, the degrading and cruel chicken industry, the plight of intelligent animals such as horses going abroad for slaughter and so it went on. The man kept up his attempt to be interested and suddenly I realised that I must stop because, as usual, whenever you are in conversation with a politician, you are really going nowhere. With great charm, this man accompanied me out of the building and really all that I had achieved was a sore throat.

Chapter **28**

GRIEF

During the summertime, Carl and Nigel, their wives and their children came to Broadhurst. The swimming pool, which I had no personal relationship with, being seriously claustrophobic and capable of becoming panic stricken even when I'm pulling my polo-neck sweater over my face, was now full of their splashing and laughter. I was always too busy to be the ideal grandma – I felt it had come to me too soon and in spite of the battering of life, I still didn't look like a grandma. However, I enjoyed these days and was always amazed to see how my once young sons were now men and their babies were now children.

After a month of screeching, laughing, dog barking, water splashing, wet feet through my house, doors slamming, fridge being emptied every five minutes, they all went home except Christopher, Nigel's fifteen-year-old son. Without doubt, Christopher and I had a special relationship. His enigmatic smile, his tall, fair-haired appearance, the sheer handsomeness of him, was something to be noticed. He invited his friend Gregory to come and stay and, for a few days, they did all the things boys do. They helped with the horses in the sanctuary, threw one another in the lake, messed about in a little boat and in the evening watched videos.

On one particular night, at about one o'clock in the morning I now know, there was a huge banging on my bedroom door. It was Gregory. He pulled no punches. 'Carla, Carla, come quick, Christopher's dead.' I can't explain the feelings as I raced along the long hall, the never-ending hall, to their bed-sit. The television was still on. Christopher was sitting with his back to me in an armchair, the clicker was on the floor by his feet. I touched him on the shoulder, 'Chris, Chris,' and very slowly and silently his body simply slid off the chair onto the floor. Greg had fled from the scene. I laid Christopher on his back and began frantic artificial respiration. I could hear myself moaning, 'Chris, Chris my darling'. I was at the wrong end of the house for a telephone. Marna and Len had not heard any of the noise. I kept pummelling and pumping him – I tried mouth to mouth. His face had gone purple. I went back to artificial respiration and because his face paled again, I thought I was winning. After a while, exhausted and knowing that I had lost, I ran back to my bedroom and phoned the police and an ambulance. I found myself sobbing and saying, 'Oh dear God, first Arragorn, now Chris'. The family were not ready for another tragedy, and Nigel, what on earth was I going to say to Nigel – so far away in Liverpool. 'Oh dear God,' I kept saying over and over again, 'Oh dear God.'

The ambulance took fifty minutes to arrive, though it would have made no difference, apparently they got lost. Marna and Len were now making coffee for them and me. I watched the ambulance men as they bent over Christopher, pumping his chest, doing all sorts of different things to him. He looked as if he were simply asleep.

Something in my brain said, 'Go and call Nigel, you can do no more.' I found the call impossible to make so my sister Marna handled it. We have never talked about what she said or what Nigel said. Our final arrival at the hospital was met by a group of medics. There were at least seven of them. There were flashing lights, a drip was set up at the end of a large trolley, everything was dark green. They came towards us, almost without making a single sound and Chris was quickly moved from the ambulance stretcher to their trolley. I stood watching it disappear along the corridor. He was dead, I knew he was dead, but the sight of those wonderful people so full of quiet purpose, taking him quickly out of sight, gave me a new but rather hopeless hope. It was a very short time before

I felt an arm around me – a lady who was not in uniform and I didn't know what role she played. 'I am so sorry,' she said, 'there was nothing we could do.'

I don't remember any more other than arriving home at dawn. The birds were beginning to sing, the sun would soon be up. There is no way of describing this kind of event. Because I was a strict vegetarian, Chris used to take sausages out of the sanctuary fridge that had been sent to us by a local butcher for the animals, and he would sneak them into my fridge. The sequence of events was always the same: I would come and find them, I would race upstairs with them, playfully hit him over the head with them, and he would pick me up and swing me round and we both would laugh. I remembered how I always used to let him drive my Mercedes up the house drive.

'What do you want to be, Chris, when you grow up?' I would ask.

A smile full of devilment would come and he would say, 'A drug dealer'. And I would playfully bash his shoulders and so it went on, and now all that, all that – gone.

Chris died of a thing called 'cardiac myopathy', rare and found in youngsters below the age of twenty. There is no cure and there is no way of knowing when they have it, unless they go for a test of some kind and it's discovered. Soon afterwards, Pandora, one of my cats died. She was Chris's favourite – he was constantly nursing her. Of all the cats I had he was always to be found with Pandora. The post mortem revealed when she died, that it was 'cardiac myopathy'.

Chapter 29

HERE WE GO AGAIN

The writing urge was back. I was restless, I felt deprived. My mind – no matter what I was doing – was being crowded with ideas and things I needed to say, so I picked up my pen and literally spilled out a one-hour play called *Our Doris*. It was a complicated story concerning a dysfunctional family set in Liverpool. Here I was on my own home ground and both drama and humour were contained in it. I felt proud of it and thought that if I were going to get back into television at all, *Our Doris* was going to do it.

I sent it to the BBC. A letter came back from the Head of Comedy, now the third in succession within a few months, saying that she loved it, it was funny and sad, just the thing they needed but they didn't do one-off plays any more. However, because they liked the play so much she was going to commission five other writers to write one-hour comedy dramas, giving her an excuse to put *Our Doris* on the screen. I was back!

The sanctuary was being run in a splendid way. I had excellent staff now and although life was filled with many other things because of the size of my house, the land and so on. I felt that now I could get my head down and go back to where I had once been.

Three curious months followed, during which I wrote a whole comedy series called *Trio*. I thought that perhaps now, rather than presenting one script, and because words were running rife in me, I would write a whole series and present it to the BBC. I was well pleased with it. It was the story of three boys who shared a flat, one of them in a wheelchair – a really terrific subject to write about. After submitting this, I sat back and thought, 'Something's got to happen – they can't hate all of it.' There was a long, long wait. I decided something I had never done, to ring the Head of Comedy and ask her if the others had written their scripts yet and whether had she received *Trio*. I found out that she had left two months before and there was no sign of any of my scripts. Nobody seemed to have seen them or know about them and, to this day, that's how it has been there.

Now I busied myself writing to government officials, MPs, heads of departments, Prince Charles and the Prime Minister. In short, I had turned to the animals again. If I couldn't save myself as a writer, I naïvely thought, I could at least save some of them. I was amazed at the support I had. Even from Prince Charles. Although he didn't actually mention live exports, I must have touched a nerve within him, because he sent me copies of some speeches he had made about animal welfare. The agricultural minister invited me to a meeting, which pleased me greatly, but the event was not worth the excitement. The subject of live exports and other matters were discussed by MAFF officials, farmers and others and I could see once again that there was no way this trade was going to end simply because the nation didn't want it. Something else was going to have to happen – and it did. BSE came along.

By now, I had set up an organisation called PAIN, which stands for Protestors' Animal Information Network. This was to be an offshoot designed to provide information for all the people who needed to be down at the docks protesting and to know the time, the place, the numbers of trucks and animals that were going out.

When winter came, very violent seas cropped up at Dover. The *Caroline*, then a small lairage ship, was carrying animals across to France, Belgium and Holland during these storms. There were rules about whether a ship should sail in certain weather, but the decision to sail was always made by the captain of the ship, who was himself part of the financial benefits of the trade. The result was that the ship always sailed.

PAIN had accumulated quite a bit of money by now and, based on everything we learned from our barrister, and our own observations, this was illegal. We decided to go to court. It was a three-day hearing. We had amassed an amazing amount of evidence against the exporters. We were given information by the Coast Guards, pilot ship captains and many others who were engaged in watching weather conditions at Dover. Supported by our barrister, we were confident that transporting animals in force 9 and 10 gales in a small ship was not only cruel but against the law as it stood.

When I entered the court and saw it full of friends and supporters and other people who, like me, had been fighting for years against this trade, I felt as though we could not lose. Our people gave their evidence clearly and dramatically. Our findings were absolute and Penny Lewis, who was our most informed and intelligent member concerning this trade, had complete confidence in the rights of this case. To my astonishment, the people chosen to defend the trade were mostly from abroad, indeed from the countries where the animals ended up. They stood in the witness box giving colourful stories of how the animals arrived in perfect condition. There was a young man who said that he had never seen a distressed animal during all the time he had worked in the trade in Belgium. Case after case of this kind was related in court.

There was a huge discussion concerning the weather, its affects on ships when crossing the Channel – they went so deeply into the subject that we were looking at charts that we could not understand. The experts rattled on about the height of waves and the depths of waves and the effect on small ships. Others spoke about the stability of the interior of the ship where the animals were – there were all kinds of so-called professional people, all with much to gain, crying for the continuation of live exports, and in spite of the remarkable case put forward by our barrister we lost. The whole thing cost PAIN a lot of money and, filled with disappointment and despair, I decided not to keep putting messages out and raising people's hopes any more. PAIN lay silent for a while but only for a while.

Chapter 30

THE SONG

During the time that I had been stamping around the various ports screeching against live exports, running my sanctuary, writing unsuccessful scripts, Linda McCartney and I had kept in touch. One day, she asked me if I had written any poetry and I said I had. She asked me to send her some and I did. On this particular day, she called me. 'I want you to come over tomorrow,' she said, 'is that possible?' She sounded bright, bright enough to make me think that a miracle was happening and that she was getting better.

'Yes,' I said, 'yes.'

'We're just having a little get-together at the studio, OK?'

'OK,' I said.

She sent a car for me. It was a bright and beautiful day and as we approached the studio which stood on a small hill, I could smell the usual Linda McCartney food and hear music. She came to greet me, taking me by the hand and towing me inside excitedly. Paul was playing his guitar and was accompanied by a wonderful sound coming from the mixing desk that was managed by his always faithful staff. Linda kept looking sideways at me.

'Listen, listen,' she said.

Paul started singing a song called 'Cow' which was one of my poems.

I couldn't believe it. He had twinned the words with a beautiful sound and then he said, 'Come on our Carla, I want you to say the chorus.'

'I can't, I can't,' I kept telling him as Linda and he managed to get me to the microphone.

'You can, you can,' they said.

What a wonderful day that was. It was a new way of getting the message out to people and here was someone as successful and as well loved as Paul liking it, and more than that, singing it. Later, Linda's LP came out and 'Cow' was one of the songs. I was so excited – at last words, words that I had written – I was coming back, I thought. But like so many dreams it shot into the sky like a firework and exploded up there. Linda had used the word 'fuck' in one of her songs. It was just before that word became acceptable anywhere and it was banned.

'Never mind,' said Linda, 'we haven't finished with them yet.'

I visited Linda often. She was still wandering about her garden taking photographs of watermelons and flowers and little things that crawled in the grass. Now and then, I caught a look of fatigue on her face. It only lasted a second and was gone, but it kept returning. We never mentioned her illness. She started to once but stopped herself and I took that to mean 'I don't really want to talk about it'.

One day she rang. 'Listen,' she said, 'I'm off to Arizona.'

'You lucky cow,' I said. 'When?'

'Now,' she said.

I could hear Paul calling. She seemed glad not to have time to say anything more.

'Listen, Carla, I'll back on the eighth, I'll see you on the ninth, OK?'

'OK,' I said.

'Have you got any chickens?'

'Yes, yes, hundreds of them.'

'Bring me some, OK, just a few for the garden.'

I drew comfort from this – she was coming back.

'Are you . . .?'

She cut in, 'Yeah, yeah, I'm fine.'

There was a strange pause. I wasn't sure whether or not she was still

Me, on holiday with 'Him' in Venice.

The American 'Producer' and me in Los Angeles.

Me with the 44 bullocks.

Me outside the stalls, in the sanctuary, part of Broadhurst Manor.

My first photograph at Broadhurst Manor – nineteen years ago!

My sister Marna, and her husband Leonard.

Me at Broahurst Manor, with Igor the 2nd.

Carl with Aeneas at his graduation from University.

Igor and me in the early days of Broadhurst Manor.

Christopher – thirteen years old – who
died at Broadhurst Manor.

Me with cats in Zoffany Heights.

My first london home with a back garden with my cats and Igor. Just out of shot – rabbits, tortoise, two home pigeons and a parrot!

Me in my first flat in Paddington, London. *The Liver Birds* finished and on to a script called *Trio* – nobody liked it so I went on to write *Bread*.

The early, young me! Posing pathetically for newspapers.

Fighting the good fight.
Me campaigning against the live exports.
The black ribbon around the post is to
commemorate the animals going abroad
for slaughter. Loud hailer hidden but at
the ready!

there, then suddenly, 'I love ya, Carla' – and she was gone.

I have spent long moments wondering whether or not she knew she would not be coming back. Only a few days later, when the press and television started ringing me, did I learn of her death. Paul came home and I, and some others, were invited to the house where we sat and talked about her, but mostly it was Paul who spoke about his deepest sorrow.

He was clearly distressed; his face was pale, his hands fidgety and now and then he gave a little nervous cough. Shortly after that, Paul held a memorial service for Linda and invited the people whom Linda had loved. Linda never pretended to like anyone, unless she really did, nor did she seek their company, and to be on her special list you had to be an animal person.

The church was literally lined with flowers and thousands of people were outside calling her name. It was a moving service during which those of us who knew her well read out our tributes to her. Later, Paul held another memorial service in New York to which I was invited. Again, it was beautifully orchestrated with people from everywhere – television, films, playwrights, poets, church people, me, cleaners, ordinary folk that she had known and loved – and it was a beautiful goodbye. I am not afraid or embarrassed to tell you that after all the talk, all the media, all the this and all the that, I was left with the feeling that she was still around and whenever anything happens regarding animals that I know she would disapprove of, I find myself raising my eyes and saying, 'They're at it again, Linda'.

'They will pay,' comes the reply.

Now more of 'Him'. He was obviously fed up with me now – his phone calls were fewer and the sanctuary was still stealing most of my time but I had excellent staff. In the past, I had had to show so many people out through that big gate – for kicking a horse, for not cleaning the aviaries properly, for not filling water bowls, for not noticing when an animal needed special care etcetera, but all those worries were over. The new problem was all the documents, all the complicated rules and regulations, tax papers, list of contributions and who made them, when they made them, invoices – bills paid, bills received – Candi and Leonard were drowning in a sea of paperwork. Also employing people was not easy – the rules for them are numerous and even more numerous are the rules for sacking someone. Not that I made a habit of this, but it is almost impossible to sack a person no matter what they do without going through weeks of investigation and more paperwork.

Also the cost of everything was going up and up. However, there was still a need in me to have this sanctuary. Because of the hundreds of animals that had passed through our hospital room doors, our knowledge was huge by now. Liz, my manageress and her staff, are capable of dealing with almost any problem that comes along and, if anything is beyond them, there is always Brian, our faithful and brilliant vet.

Amid all this my writing heart started beating again. I longed for the days of writing, rehearsals, filming, and that joy of all joys – the studio night. The BBC had changed so. Once I visited the BBC to do an interview. After it was over, I wandered round the old places, past the old Head of Comedy's office. The door was slightly open. I knocked, there was no reply and so I pushed it further open. A man sat with his back to me – he was totally at one with the computer.

'Oh hello,' I said, 'sorry.'

He didn't speak but stretched his hand out behind him towards me to save him giving any form of greeting. A large yucca plant beside his desk painfully reached for the light from the window but was dying in the process.

'Your yucca plant is dying?' I said.

There was no reply so I took a paper cup from one of the desks and went to the nearest bathroom, took it back to the office, poured it as noisily as I could onto the yucca plant. There was no response. I left.

I treated myself to a coffee downstairs. I sat watching girls, who seemed to be dressed for nightclubbing rather than working at the BBC. As I was thinking these thoughts, a group of three of them stood in front of me and there was a little whispering going on. Eventually one of them broke free and came to me.

'Excuse me,' she said, 'are you Carla Lane?'

'I am,' I said.

She held out her hand. 'Oh, I'm so pleased to meet you.' She called to the others, 'It is her, it is her.'

They all shook my hand, giggled a lot and departed. This happened two or three more times, people coming up to me asking me if I were Carla Lane. I started to think that perhaps I wasn't, and I was struck by the great, yawning gap between what was happening there now and what had once happened. There was a sense of comradeship once upon a time – the producers of programmes and heads of departments were mature and were expected to be. Here, the seeds of youth grew strong and, in spite of the fact that I had admitted to being Carla Lane many times, I sat in that little café with my cold cup of coffee feeling totally irrelevant.

One morning, I received a phone call from the sanctuary. It simply said, 'You'd better get here quickly.'

I was weak with dread as I hurried over. I thought, 'The horses have escaped, the stables have collapsed, there's been a fire, there are dead animals lying all over the paddock.'

But not so.

The yard was full of people, new people, farmers in fact, and by the look of them, well-off farmers. The yard was littered with their horseboxes and various animals carriers. Before I could say anything, somebody took me by my sleeve to a stable. There were twenty-four tiny calves, maybe four weeks old, all staring at me. He ushered me into another stable with another twenty tiny calves. The farmers had brought them to my sanctuary as a protest – they had also brought the press with them because they needed a name to link their protest to. I never did discover what their protest was about as I was simply too delighted to see the calves. They were so beautiful and so vulnerable, and I felt that I could cope with them. The next day, the papers were full of the needs of farmers, and some explanation as to why they had brought these calves to my sanctuary. There were pictures of me surrounded by farmers and calves and it all brought a tiny bit of excitement into my despondency.

The first week was fun. They were lovely sunny days. We made a boundary around the yard and the calves had access to the big barn and they skipped and cavorted around and I began to think, 'I can cope with all this.' Very soon we were plunged into various unexpected expenses. We needed things like feeding troughs especially designed for young calves, masses of straw, proper fencing to keep them within the yard and a special milk powder which was £4 a bag and they consumed ten of these a day. Mayhem had arrived. I called a great friend of mine, Dick White, who was a brilliant vet. 'What do I do with them?' I asked.

'You castrate them, you dehorn them, you worm them . . .' He paused. 'I'll see you tomorrow,' he said.

The next day, the sanctuary yard looked like a battlefield. Each barn housed several calves being castrated at a time. Dick's staff, all dressed in their green, were racing from barn to barn carrying various 'weapons'. Next was the dehorning. This was a somewhat more alarming process. The horn buds have to be burnt out – the smell was awful. One could easily imagine that the whole place was being burnt down. The calves themselves lay around, heavy eyed, with Dick chasing from one to the other, checking that they were managing. Finally, the sound of Dick's voice: 'All balls off.'

That evening they were lying quietly in the barns, looking as if nothing had happened. I went to bed quite pleased with the day and indeed, began to look forward to the next day.

The first thing I noticed was that already the calves seemed to have grown taller, fatter and lethal. When we set up the milk-feeding trough, there was a great siege. All of them ran at it, knocking us over, pushing and shoving – at one point, all I could see of one of my staff was a pair of wellies protruding from a mountain of hay. Their strength was unbelievable. It took us ages to separate them and put them in small numbers to feed together in different stables. That day gave me an insight into the fact that this was not going to be all fun. They were growing quickly and there simply wasn't room in our yard for all forty-four of them, and all our other paddocks and stables were full. The obvious thing I had to do was to try and find a temporary place for them before they wrecked the entire sanctuary.

I was lucky with this. A lady whom I knew nearby had a huge open sided barn. She said I could house the calves in it. Catching them and transporting them was just another nightmare but finally we had them safely housed in this lovely barn. But there was another problem. The barn needed special plastic sheeting all round it to stop wind and rain coming in. This was an enormous and expensive job. It was all hands on deck, but at the end of a few days the task was done, and now the calves were safe, I thought, but I was wrong. Soon, they were quite easily jumping the rail and running amok round the neighbourhood. These little chaps were now taking all our time, all our money, all our patience and I had no idea where it was all going. The one good thing was that Paul had offered to provide me with hay and straw for them and he does so to this day.

I decided to try and find a farmer who would look after them, so I put out an article in the local papers. The phone never stopped – I was impressed. But there was a hiccup. Each farmer, one after the other, muttered almost the same sentence to me: 'I'll mind them until their thirty months is up.' What they were saying was that 'then they go for slaughter and the subsidies are due'. This was not the plan – slaughter was not on the agenda. Every day, I received at least a dozen phone calls, but all of them were obsessed with the words 'slaughter' and 'subsidies'.

And then came a new voice over the phone. 'I'm a farmer, I live close by – I'll look after your bullocks for you. The thing is . . .'

'I know. You want the subsidies.'

'No,' he said, 'no. I'll mind them for you.'

'For how long?' I asked.

'As long as you want.'

Enter David Kemp, a local farmer, who took on these delinquents with ease and understanding. The cost would be £1,300 a month in the winter and a little less in the summer. They were dispatched to a beautiful green valley, close to my sanctuary, there to graze and that was the beginning of the lives of these forty-four tiny bullocks who now stand between six and eight feet high.

Now I cross the fields with David and look forward to my visit and to the sight of them coming up over the hill and galloping towards us. The scene is like an ever-changing oil painting. They do not stop to graze but, obeying David's amazing dogs, they come charging and snorting – sometimes one feels that they are not going to stop, but they do – and they thrust their great heads, pushing you aside, some of them collide their fat pink lips with your face and they tug at your hair – every one a gentleman. Well, except one of them, who seemed to regard me as a mate. I felt too enormous feet on my shoulders and it felt as if a tractor had parked on my back. To keep my balance, I grabbed hold of the side of my car while David shouted and pushed him away. I kept telling myself that I should be flattered and that here was a bullock with good taste.

David is different from most farmers that I know. He had come from a religious background – his father having been a minister. He seems to have two needs – to care for animals and to rear them for the purpose of meat – in other words, he has great compassion but he also owns the bravery needed to send them away. David doesn't bullshit. His philosophy is undaunted. He will show me proudly his prize bull and while I am almost on my knees in awe of this enormous beast, who stands with head lowered, front feet apart, great challenging eyes and quivering nose, he says quietly 'Aye, he goes on Friday'.

I burst out passionately, 'How could you David? How could you send this most wonderful beast to slaughter? How?'

He answers quietly, 'I'm a farmer.'

Chapter **31**

COMINGS AND GOINGS

I still had a serious money problem – the sanctuary was growing ever larger. I had to install a small office in the house for Candi and Leonard. Slowly it was all becoming very business-like, the very thing I dreaded most. Candi, who could type and manage the computer – all the things that I was incapable of – made life much easier and soon she had a file for this and a file for that, and Animaline was running smoothly with Leonard doing the boring financial bits.

One day I get a phone call from a good friend, John.

'Have you read about the six shire-horses?'

'No,' I said, 'no I haven't.'

'Well, there are six shires. They belonged to various brewers but are now obsolete.' He added dramatically, 'They're going to be slaughtered, Carla.'

'How much?' I asked.

'They want six thousand pounds for them.'

With my usual lack of ability to be serious about money matters, I said immediately: 'Fine, we'll go halves.'

John arranged it all. The young horses went to a sanctuary, and two of the older males, Jimmy and Charlie, and the younger female, Octavia – a more thoughtful name I felt – came to us. What amazing creatures they are – huge, proud and so gentle. They go out of their way to avoid treading or bumping into you. Nothing looks more splendid than a shire-horse, with its coat shining in the sun and great tail thrashing from side to side, feet which look as though they weigh a ton each, and then the sudden gentle, almost dainty trot to the water trough. As usual, I was saddled with certain problems. Jimmy developed a very serious foot deformity and we had to have specially made canvas boots for him. How funny he looked. But they did the trick and soon his feet were strong enough again to carry his great body.

During those days, apart from many horses, we had donkeys and Shetlands, too, and one day the then manager came to me and said, 'There's an old lady to see you.'

I met her in the sanctuary yard. She was with her daughter, who said, 'My mother is not very well – she has a horse which she loves dearly and she wants it to come to your sanctuary.'

I was immediately stricken with worry – we could not afford any more horses, we did not have any room for more horses and yet this dear, frail lady looked at me in a way which almost forced me to say 'We'll take your horse, don't worry', and so we did. I had to have another stable built to cope with overcrowding. A few months later, I got a lovely letter from the old lady saying how pleased she was and grateful and how it made, what seemed to be the end of her life, a much happier time, knowing that her horse was being cared for. Shortly after that her daughter rang and said, 'Carla, my mother has died, but because of your kindness to the horse she loved she has remembered you in her will.'

I was saddened by her death, but delighted to be receiving money for the sanctuary which was always in great need.

Several months later, the manager of the sanctuary came to me and said, 'I've got good news and bad news. The good news is that the old lady's will has now been settled.'

'Oh good,' I said.

'And the bad news is, she's left you another bloody horse.'

The infrequent phone calls between 'Him' and me now consisted of the inevitable 'How are you?' and 'I'm fine', ending with 'OK, I'll see you, bye'. I felt that all the passion we had had over the years had run as dry as a summer stream. The mayhem of the sanctuary prevented me from thinking of anything else, and because he did not phone me very much I was allowing the whole escapade to fade away. When I saw couples wandering round the countryside surrounding me, I wondered what on earth was the matter with us. We were incapable of living together, incapable of not living together – just incapable.

One morning my phone rang, the voice of one of my staff said, 'There is a dead fox lying on the lawn.' It bore several bite wounds and had somehow got away. It had been dead for quite a while and I realised that it had been hunted, and that I was living among people who didn't like me – probably because I was against pheasant shooting, lamping, snaring – all the things they did on the land surrounding me. When we moved the fox, there was a crumpled note beneath him – it read, 'Ha, ha, here's one you couldn't save.' I was unable to pretend that the sound of the hunting horn unnerved me. I tried to keep telling myself that we are all kinds and I couldn't expect the entire world to be my kind, but this fox, with its gruesome message, told me that I was not welcome and it frightened me.

'His' car had arrived outside the main gates of the house. I was glad to see him. We held hands and walked towards the sanctuary. I hoped that this time he would come to terms with what we do and why we're here and perhaps see in the animals something beautiful, which was a word he had not applied to them so far. His objections began immediately as he ballet danced across a sea of mud.

From there we journeyed from the 'Just ignore him, he won't hurt', to 'Take no notice of him, he won't touch you', to 'Just walk round him and he won't notice', to him finally holding aloft a severely mauled finger. This injury had been delivered by Joe, the goose guard, who maims everybody, especially when their backs are turned.

'He doesn't mean it,' I explained, 'he's a goose with a past. He's tarnished by his experiences.'

'So am I,' he muttered.

Somehow or other this accident-prone man managed to arrive at the house, where my two dogs and ten cats greeted him. It was an avalanche of paws, teeth, miaows and barks. I explained, 'Look, they love you.' I guided him carefully to the more gentle beings like the canary and budgie aviary, the rabbit hutches. He actually picked one of these up and murmured, 'Oh, they're all floppy, aren't they?' Still I thought, 'not very profound but it's a beginning.'

We spent the night together to the sound of a queue of cats and dogs holding a protest outside the bedroom door. We had breakfast to the sounds of singing canaries, talking parrots and the sound of Wolfgang using his litter tray.

Chapter 32

ONCE UPON A TIME

Roy came to my sanctuary to campaign for funds for us. He was in his early forties, a brilliant guitarist, and had a rather posh, Air Force officer's accent. At that time the cottage belonging to the manor house was empty and as Roy was recommended to me by the Colonel, a very dear and important friend to us both, I was happy for him to live there. At first, I found him to be rather loud, a bit overpowering, a bit strenuous, but as he settled down I could see somewhere in him a sad, lonely person. He had been a qualified hospital nurse and had a great knowledge of human illness – often his knowledge became invaluable in our sanctuary hospital room, as he helped to administer injections and things of that kind.

For a few months his attempts to make funds for us were unsuccessful and I could see that this was worrying him deeply. Loud, confident Roy was disappearing. He had become quieter, more reserved – no longer standing in the yard of the sanctuary at seven in the morning with a cup of coffee in his hand heralding the incoming birds, but rather staying in his cottage and now and then inviting staff to have a coffee with him. I knew by now that here was the loneliest man. He had an estranged wife and two children who lived in Spain. His brother had died. He seemed, though, to have many intellectual friends – most of whom came to visit him at the sanctuary. They were pleasant and some of them were important.

One evening, I received a phone call from the local police. A voice said, 'Did you know you had someone injured on your premises?'

I told them that no, I didn't know that.

'Well he's phoned here,' he said, 'he's asked for an ambulance. He said that he's made it to the cottage.'

I raced there. Roy was lying on the floor between the kitchen and the lounge of the cottage. There was a sizeable pool of blood on the carpet and I noticed a rifle propped up against the fridge.

'Roy, Roy – what on earth has happened?'

He spoke in a pained whisper. 'I saw a rat in the kitchen – tried to shoot it.'

I didn't listen for any more. I fled to the house to find Andy the gardener. He and Emma were watching television. I asked Andy to go and he did. He came back later saying that he had called an ambulance and that the police had come and gone. Roy was in hospital for a week. He had ripped open a vein in his chest and was lucky to have survived. I was never ever sure about believing what he said, particularly as the rifle was propped up. If it had happened the way he had explained, then the rifle would have been abandoned on the floor. It is almost inconceivable that a rat could be in his kitchen – it was so well guarded against them and we didn't have many anyway. I decided not to be too dramatic about this and to accept what he told me.

When he came from the hospital, Roy was very quiet. He hardly ever came out of the cottage, gone was the loud Air Force voice – the loud laughter – the loud greeting. And then he called me and said, 'I am going to stay with a couple of friends,' and he named them and I knew them and I felt that this would be helpful to him.

During those evenings when I was on duty in the hospital room and on my way back to the house each night, I had to pass the cottage. He had left some lights on and I thought that was OK and for three nights I just passed the cottage thinking, 'Oh, he's not back yet.' On the fourth night, I began to think that I ought to investigate to see if everything was all right in there. I didn't expect the door to be open but it was, and when I went inside I noticed an obnoxious smell.

'Oh,' I thought, 'he's left something in the fridge.'

But he hadn't.

'It must be somewhere in the cottage,' I thought.

I walked through the little lounge, looking vaguely, and into the bedroom which was gently lit by the lamps in the sanctuary yard. At the head of the bed, I noticed a bin bag which seemed full of clothes. I thought, 'Oh, he's left some washing. I'll put it in the machine for him,' which I sometimes did. I pulled the bedclothes back a little in order to pick up the bag and in the dim yellow light I saw his blackened body. He was lying on his side and his hand was frozen into a strange shape and sticking out beyond him towards me. I fled from the cottage back to the house calling Andy again. Emma, his partner, made me a cup of coffee and Andy went to see what had happened.

Once again Broadhurst Manor was encumbered with police cars, ambulance, other vehicles and white-suited men. Andy, Emma and I sat quietly in the kitchen of Broadhurst and now and then an officer would come and tell us what the findings were. At first, they thought he had been murdered but after two or three visits they came and announced that they had found a drug and several other items beneath his bed and it was now clear that he had committed suicide.

It was weeks before I could even pass the cottage again – I had to go the long way round to get to the sanctuary. I kept remembering the night he died. He had called me into the cottage and needed to talk. I started to tell him how lucky he was, the way he looked, his musical talent, his ability to be noticed. 'You have so much going for you, Roy. It doesn't matter if you haven't made money for the sanctuary – neither has anybody else. It's not an easy thing to do.' I also reminded him that once he was an alcoholic and now he wasn't. 'That,' I said, 'is one of the hardest things for a human being to do, and you did it.' He was not a tactile man and, for the one and only time, he gave me a gentle hug and simply said, 'Thank you Carla.' I thought I had won.

A few days later, 'Him' was back. I was stealing a couple of days off and he was sitting in his car waiting for me to join him. We were going to a little hotel that we knew in the early days to celebrate the fact that we hadn't quarrelled for a week. Just as I was rushing out to his car, my phone rang. I rushed back intending to be but a moment. It was a good friend who had sold one of his paintings and wanted to send the money to my sanctuary. I hadn't seen him for such a long time and we talked for quite a while, and when I went back to the car 'He' was sitting hunched up, full of anger, the engine running and a face that looked as if it were contemplating suicide.

'I'm sorry,' I babbled, 'it was a good friend.'

Silence.

'I'm sorry,' I said again, 'I can't ignore these people – they want to help my sanctuary.'

Silence.

I couldn't stop my voice from rising slightly.

'Besides, I like talking to this person.'

Silence.

'And why shouldn't I talk to whomever I like?'

Silence.

'I don't tell you who to talk to, do I?'

He turned the engine off.

'Oh, I see,' I mimicked. 'I'd better turn the engine off – this could go on for ever.'

Silence.

And then: 'Why didn't you tell him you were on your way out?'

'Because I didn't want to.'

He started the car and we went just a few yards. I shrieked at him, 'It was only ten minutes for God's sake.'

He reversed the few yards back, I got out of the car, so did he. He walked slowly, slowly – like an actor in a 1920s' film – and we passed the garden pond. I noticed the fish lounging on the surface. I pointed to a large golden coloured fish.

'I've had him for fifteen years,' I whispered trying to break the silence.

'Poor chap,' came the reply.

He walked back to his car. I didn't follow. He got in and switched the engine on.

'I'll teach him,' I thought. 'I'll show him. He thinks I'm going to run after him, but I'm not.'

He drove off – I was mortified. I wanted to shout up the lane after him 'You bastard, you selfish bastard, you . . .'.

Over the next few days I had to find a way to quell the anger I felt towards him. After all, he wasn't the most verbal of lovers – one had to guess so much – and I am up front, all things said, poetically if possible, but if that fails then I get to the raw verbal stuff. I decided to compose a letter. It made gentle comments about his lack of enthusiasm concerning our relationship, about the way he came and went like a little stream causing all things to grow, then recoiling leaving no more than mud. I was quite proud of my letter. I got as far as signing it and putting it in an envelope, and then I realised that he probably would not really know what I was talking about, so I didn't send it.

Chapter 33

LOOKING BACK

I was wandering around the house and I came upon my various awards. They were almost hidden by little plants sitting in front of them, brought about I hope, by modesty. I found myself almost tearful at the sight of them; each one represented wonderful moments in my life, times when I was doing what I wanted to do and what I could do – successful times. Each one brought to my mind the sound of applause, of acknowledgement, of those terrifying walks from the stage to the table. I stood and looked at them for a long time, listening to the speeches, the laughter.

And all the other writers of my time, where were they? Were they standing gazing at their awards – I could hear the voices of their work inside my head: the wonderful sound of Captain Mainwaring in *Dad's Army*, a little man with huge ambitions who tried to be proper at all times, a variety of charges in his care, each one with a distinct personality, with failures and weaknesses which we all recognise and yet he rose above them with modest dignity; *'Allo, 'Allo* with the café owner who was surrounded by a posse of failed people – a wife whose voice would cause a tree to uproot itself, a gay man – never offensive but without doubt he was truly gay – the frilly, cuddly, barmaid who gave René something to live for (haven't we all met these people?); *Steptoe and Son* – a man trying to rise above the shambles of his life as a rag-and-bone man, but who was hampered by his old-fashioned, cantankerous father. Throughout it all one felt the great love they had for each other and so the series could hold, without injury, the many, almost savage, arguments. And so many more coming from our screens, with everything we knew and understood containing that God-given magic which made us laugh – never to return.

Things had become so different. Comedy had journeyed through a stage of being about real, recognisable situations, with scenes and words which people could associate with. Suddenly, it was plunged into something quite different; this difference being called 'reality'. While we, the comedy writers of the past, tried to inject reality into our scripts, the real reality is painful, harsh, unattractive and boring. We have bad kids, fat people, makeovers, dysfunctional families – these subjects do not fall lightly on our screen – we are watching human beings at their lowest ebb, their most vulnerable and in some cases, their most disgusting.

At first, this new concept was interesting but now we have to watch cameras zooming in on hanging breasts, big stomachs, bad teeth, anger, foul language – all the things which we already know about and which are not the entirety of the human beings portrayed. For a while, I found myself tolerating it, but now I quickly switch to another channel. It's not that I don't have compassion for these people – I feel sad for anyone who is suffering in any way, be it that their dog is biting them, that their husbands are too fat to be attractive or that their kids are telling them to 'f*** off'. In my own life, there have been things which have not been the way I would want them, but I would find it impossible to unleash all the terrible crevices in my makeup just for money, and until now my stretch marks have always remained a secret.

I read in the paper one day that the head of a vivisection laboratory had received an OBE. This angered me. I have seen animals in laboratories. I can imagine a trusting paw being offered to the white-coated men as they perform horrifying experiments, and I cannot bear to think of animals being cheated and hurt in this way – so I sent my OBE back.

I received a letter from Tony Blair about its return; it was handwritten. It ended with, 'I am sorry that you have returned your OBE. I feel that you deserve it and I will keep it here until you want it back.'

Chapter 34

HENRY, RUPERT & THE REST

Once again, my major worry was finance. Our horses, Henry and Rupert, developed problems. Henry had colic, which, though common in a horse, can lead to disaster. At the same time, the big ginger cob had tests that discovered cancer behind one of his eyes. Henry became worse and Rupert's treatment became urgent. Both had to enter an equine clinic where they would receive the special care they needed. One night, just after midnight, I received a call to say that Henry needed an urgent operation, and the following morning I received a phone call to say that Rupert's eye needed removing. There followed days of anxiety but soon both the horses were returned to the sanctuary in good health.

The total cost was £8000. In order to pay this, we had to take out a bank loan. When our next newsletter went out and we informed our members of what had happened, to our astonishment we were deluged with donations, each one accompanied by a little message: 'For Rupert and Henry – I hope the horses get well', 'Our thoughts are with Rupert and Henry' etcetera. The black cloud was lifted. We paid back the money to the bank and there was enough left for us to go forwards without any immediate panic. Henry recuperated well. Rupert came back to us without the slightest concern about the fact that he now had only one eye, it didn't seem to affect him at all, and now, after three years of waiting, we were told that the cancer had not spread.

The time had come for me to phone 'Him' and pour out all the thoughts I had accumulated about our so-called relationship. I sat by the phone with a strong cup of coffee and as soon as he picked up the phone, I said, 'I don't think you and I are right for each other.'

Nothing.

'I mean, normal relationships actually see each other every day – in fact, they live together, they sleep in the same bed. Not now and then, but every night.'

Nothing.

'I think we should end it.'

Nothing.

'I'm going now.'

Nothing.

'Bye.'

Nothing.

I put the phone down. I thought, 'That went really well.'

There came a moment when I had to write, I just had to write. I had to get away from television. I was sitting beside my fishpond watching all the gold and yellow fish basking peacefully, when I heard a loud 'moo' from a distant field. I began to ask myself questions: 'How does a cow feel?' 'When he's grazing, is he happy, is he unaware of the difference of day and night, and when does fear come?' That was it; I knew now that I was going to write a book called *The Dancing Cow*.

The need to do this was irreversible. A huge tidal wave of words followed that – first, I had to ask myself, 'What do you mean – a dancing cow?' This question was answered almost before it was asked. 'The cow is frightened because he has been asked to enter a truck which he feels is evil. Although he was used to going into trucks, he thought, 'This is different and he found himself up on his two hind legs, turning and turning to keep his balance, it looked as if he were dancing.'

Excitement grew. I hadn't talked to anybody about it, but now I had created a host of other animals that shared a large barn with Flo, the dancing cow: Isaac the intelligent spider, a depressed beetle, geese, chickens, pigs and, I suppose, the favourite character for me, the rat. Now my pen was in my hand, I couldn't stop – every single word fell out and in one week the book was finished.

I sent it to Paul just to ask him to read it and he wrote back: 'Carla Lane is a passionate defender of animals and their interests. She is their friend and, incidentally, my friend, too. Her writing contains all her passion, laced with pathos and humour. *The Dancing Cow* is funny, witty and at the same time, a vision of a better world.'

Since my life simply has to be dotted with dramas and things going right are seldom allowed, I had reached a comfortable feeling that things going right had now arrived. *The Dancing Cow* was being considered by a publisher; the sanctuary had earned and was receiving a good name; my sons were phoning me daily, painting idyllic pictures of their lives, the lives of the ladies they had finally ended up with and their resulting children, and I had received an almost loving call from 'Him', though not the kind of loving that most people would recognise and it was more in the sound of the voice than in the words spoken. So feeling good, I took my two dogs for a walk.

It was a beautiful summer's evening, about eight o'clock, as we wandered along lanes, across fields, through the water splash and by the time we reached home it was just beginning to grow dusk. The two large gates at the entrance to Broadhurst Manor have a piece of metal which protrudes from the path to guide them when to stop and start. I had pressed my clicker and they were opening and, as they did so, I squeezed through before they were wide open, and tripped over that piece of metal. I had a dog lead in each hand and I went crashing to the ground. I felt the whole of my face hit the stone path and for a moment I just lay there. The dogs stood quietly, whining gently and when I lifted my face I could actually hear the blood dripping onto the stone. I was not in any actual pain and managed to get to my feet and start walking to the house. But then I felt my sweater was wet and warm and panic overtook me. I ran to the cottage, but there was no one there, so I ran to the house and straight to the kitchen phone and rang Marna and Len who were in their flat upstairs. The dogs were shifting nervously beneath the table and for the first time I saw just how much blood I was losing. It seemed to be everywhere – all over the floor, smeared against the kitchen cupboards, in the kitchen sink, all round the telephone.

'Oh my God,' said Marna, as she came in, 'oh my God, what have you done?'

Len was in her wake.

From what I remember they picked up a big towel and pressed it against my face and Leonard steered me out of the room into his car.

At the hospital, the question from each nurse was, 'What have you been doing?' The deepest cut was on my cheek beneath my left eye – there was a jagged scrape on my forehead and chin – my nose had a gash the full length of it and it looked as if it had burst in the middle, and there were several other nasty little marks. I was cleaned up, given another appointment and taken home, and by then the real pain had begun. My lips swelled up and particularly my forehead, which, though it was the least injured part, hurt me the most. They had said in the hospital that there were a couple of tiny pebbles embedded in it, which they had removed.

Any woman reading this will know the fears I had. They were of this horrendously disfigured lady who frightened to death everybody she encountered, who could no longer afford to have a camera looking her way and who, if she were sensible, should book into a monastery. It took six weeks for my technicolour appearance to disappear. My nose gathered itself together very cleverly, each cut had turned into a fine red line and the bruising was now moving from black to ochre. I had lived for six weeks being greeted by every person with the words 'Oh my God'. This is a phrase which I heard more than any other, and it is also one which I use more than any other, but one thing I did think at the time, when finally my face healed, was that a slight restoration seemed to have occurred, which brought about the same look that an old cupboard has when it has been planed and repainted.

Chapter 35

THE GATHERING

There was to be a great gathering in New York of animal people and some awards were to be given out. Celia Hammond, a lady for whom I have so much admiration, who was once a beautiful model who willingly gave that position away so that she could care tirelessly for cats, and I decided to go to this gathering together, and we booked into a hotel near Canal Street. During this pleasant evening, an award was given to Paul for his concern about animals. He held it high and said to the crowd, 'I share this with Linda.'

On my return from New York, Marna and Len tried to make me take a break.

'Oh for goodness' sake,' said Marna, 'ring 'Him' up and go off the pair of you. Have a nice time. I'm sick of you now.'

It was two months since I had last seen 'Him' – he had driven away from Broadhurst with the speed of a fire engine. I almost hated him, but over the weeks I began to remember his fine face, his rare smile, the way he walked and the way he brought irritation, frustration and great passion into my life. As I was thinking about this he called me.

'Hello,' he said.

'Hello.'

'Are you all right?'

'Yes, I'm fine.'

'It's been a long time.'

'Yes.'

'Are you all right?' (He'd already asked me that.)

'Yes.'

'Are you coming up to London at all?' (Play hard to get.)

'Well, not really.'

'Give me a call then.'

'I will, yes.'

'OK,' and he put the phone down.

After half a minute, I grabbed the phone and found myself saying 'You said give you a call.'

'Yes, yes I did.'

'Let's go somewhere – somewhere far away.'

'OK, where do you want to go?'

I didn't really know where I wanted to go, but . . . 'Venice,' I said.

We booked into the most expensive hotel in Venice and our room overlooked the Grand Canal. We made a plan – a plan that would involve us both trying to forget everything but the fact that our journey might enable us to be sane and sensible.

For a few days things were ecstatic. We wandered into splendid churches with carvings, oil paintings, inscriptions, polished pews and great Gothic stones. We visited the markets and stood in awe of the great bell tower in St Mark's Square. Now the simple fact was that by that time I wanted a cup of tea. It obviously did not match his needs, as we passed endless tea and coffee shops, but he didn't show any sign of slowing down. We were now in another church. I love churches, but I now felt I had seen enough of them so I whispered, 'I'm dying for a cup of tea.'

He seemed not to hear me – he was running his hand over carved wood and saying 'Isn't this amazing'. I agreed with him – it was amazing but it was becoming less amazing because of my desperate need for that cup of tea. Sensing another row, and in a bid to stop it developing, I said, 'Now look, why don't you wander off and see the things you want to? I'll wander off and see the things I want to,' and I added, 'and have a cup of tea.'

So, we ended up going in different directions. He wandered about looking at the beautiful statues and bridges, and I wandered up and down the Grand Canal looking at the same things, only from a boat.

As we were leaving Venice, we both knew that our story was coming to its end. I could already feel that my relationship with 'Him' had grown pale with exhaustion. We were both reaching out for different things now. Each time we met, we ended up conducting a post mortem on the once magic, once passionate time that we had had. But we could never find anything that could rescue it from what seemed now to be the beginning of its end. We didn't mention the word 'goodbye' – instead we were both full of 'See you soon', 'Take care', 'I'll call you', ending with a long, long pause, each waiting for the other to walk away.

Not long ago, I decided to have a party – a sort of gesture to all my friends before my money ran out completely. A big beautiful, memorable party – like the ones I used to have at Zoffany House only more so. I would invite all the people I knew and had somehow along the way lost.

Marna and Len were pleased by the idea and, very shortly, all the invitations were sent out. Some vegetarian friends were going to cook for me, other friends were going to do the drinks, and Broadhurst Manor was filled with a feverish anticipation.

It was a bright and beautiful day. I hired lots of little tables and chairs with bright umbrellas and yellow tablecloths to be placed about the sunken garden and the terrace outside the main back door of the house. I arranged for a lady to play the harp in the hallway so that it could be heard both inside and outside. I called in a firm to provide glasses, dishes and all things to do with food. All was set.

The only people who were not going to be there were my sons who were both on holiday with their children. In the past I had had many get-togethers, but this one was going to be the best. I invited everybody I could think of – those who played in all the shows that I had written and those who were involved in the production side; those who had helped me with my sanctuary and its beginnings; a little, valued crowd from Liverpool and a posse of well-known actors and actresses. The atmosphere was fantastic. The voices of all kinds of people filtered through the air as they greeted each other, laughed and joked with each other and related stories to each other of their successes and failures – all to the tune of a harp.

The first little hiccup came when I met my friend Jenny Seagrove rushing along the upstairs hall with a bowl full of water in her hand and her dog at her heels.

'The cistern above the toilet is leaking,' she said. 'I've been trying to rescue it.'

I pointed her in the direction of one of the many other toilets and called Alan, the handyman at the sanctuary.

Suddenly, there was a great noise coming from the hall. A young, up-and-coming actor had punched a vet.

'You take money from people to cure their animals,' said the actor.

Another guest said, 'He's a vet, darling. He has to be paid for the work he does, like you.'

'I don't harm animals,' he said.

'Neither does he,' said the quiet voice.

As the vet was in the process of lifting himself off the floor, the actor prepared for a second attack. So I called Alan to separate them.

Not many minutes later, Michael Angelis came very discreetly to me and said, 'You'd better come quickly – some people taken the dinghy out and it's capsized. They're both in the lake.'

As we spoke, the wet and bedraggled pair (whom like so many others shall remain nameless!), one of them still holding their wine glass, approached us. They were a little shocked but they were also a little drunk and none of it mattered. I called Alan.

Later, I overheard a little conversation between Michael Winner and one of the actors from *Bread*: 'Oh,' said the slightly merry actor, 'the last time I saw you was at the theatre – *Fiddler on the Roof*.'

'Oh,' retorted the slightly merry Michael, 'that's strange. I've never seen *Fiddler on the Roof*.'

I decided to let that one go and I went out into the grounds to see if all was well there. It was one of the happiest little moments, watching all the people I had loved and worked with – Chrissie, my typist and production assistant on *Bread*, Rita Tushingham, Lynsey de Paul and Jeff Beck, who so often visited my house and each time in a different vintage car. My garden was ringing with their laughter and beautifully told stories, the food was sumptuous – an almost perfect day.

While all this was happening, a complete stranger to me was going round running his finger over the furniture and muttering: 'No dust, no fuckin' dust.' I decided to leave him. In the library, a little group of young people, whom I didn't know, were sitting. This was to be my first experience of gatecrashers. Their conversation consisted of: 'Oh yeah, man, wow, yeah – that is beautiful, wow, yeah, man.'

'Excuse me,' I said in my nicest tone, 'I'd like you to leave, if you don't mind. We're a bit overcrowded here and I don't know you, and I think . . .'

'Fuck off,' said one of them.

I called Alan.

Then I received a phone call. One of my guests was lying prone in the lane leading to my house. He was calling out 'Julie, Julie, I love you Julie.' Alan called through the loudhailer – 'Is there anyone here called Julie?'

A lady stepped forwards. 'My name is Julie,' she said.

Alan said discreetly, 'I believe there's someone looking for you in the lane.'

'Who?' she asked.

'I don't know who he is. He's young and, and, er, has dark hair, and he's drunk. He said his name was Eddie.'

'Oh, that's my husband – he always does this – I'll pick him up on the way home,' she said.

I was suddenly made aware of the fact that a taxi had been called to pick up one of the guests who was going to go and pick up another guest. Apparently, the guest was getting in the taxi one side and getting straight out the other. The driver said, 'I can't cope with him. He keeps walking through my taxi – he's bloody barmy.'

Alan saw to it.

Later in the day, when all was calm, all the agitators had fallen into a drunken sleep and everybody was just talking about old times, about things they had done, adventures they had had. It was very peaceful, very colourful and it was something I would have liked 'Him' to have witnessed. Most of the people there would have known him and he would have had a great time, but it wasn't to be. A certain amount of chaos ensued at night-time. There was so much food left over that we handed out little parcels to people of what they called their favourite thing. The girls who did it for me finished their job round about eight o'clock that night, and I went upstairs to get the £700 I had put aside to pay them – it had gone. There was no point in calling Alan.

After an horrendous amount of washing and tidying up, the house was back to normal. The cats had come out of hiding, the parrots began to talk and shout again, the canaries began to sing, the dogs wandered round feasting on crumbs and anything else they could find, and finally I climbed wearily into bed. I was awoken by the phone ringing. I switched the light on and looked at the clock. It was nearly half past one in the morning. My heart began to race – were my sons all right, had anything happened that I didn't know about, had anybody been killed on the way home – or was it 'Him'? Out of habit, I put on my sexiest voice and said, 'Hello.'

The voice said, 'Is that the Chinese takeaway?'

Chapter 36

FEELING SAFE

We are now near the end of the book. I have told you as much as I can remember, but I can already see that for years to come, I will keep thinking, 'Oh, I should have put that in my book', especially when I remember that I have been visited by a few catastrophes not mentioned, mainly because I came out of them safe and sound. I was, for instance, in Harrods when the bomb went off there; I was in Los Angeles when they had their worst earthquake; I was in New York when John Lennon was killed, and with my friend Celia, I had just set foot on a plane leaving New York as the events of 9/11 unfolded.

Carl and Nigel are proving to be what I call 'decent folk'. We have never allowed life to separate us. They are my dearest friends and my reasons for feeling safe. My beautiful grandchildren have now changed from being babies to grown-ups. I almost began to write more pages concerning their many achievements, but I felt that as you have got this far in the book, you deserve a break. Enough to say, all of them are little print-outs of me, that is because their fathers were also little print-outs of me and the print-out says, 'Don't let the earwigs drown in the dog dish'.

Three years ago, Claremont was turned into luxury flats. I went to gaze at it one more time. The façade had been saved, the old stable yard is now a modern garden but the twisting drive leading up to the entrance is still there, just as it was. I could hear the sound of family days – it always seemed to be summer at Claremont – and the same little patch of grass where Egor is buried is unharmed and remarkably the same, rather tatty, little rose tree is still trying to bloom there.

Now my solace is walking round the gardens of Broadhurst Manor. I count myself as more than fortunate. The great oak trees, the tall grass, the four lakes and the wild flowers are all home to every creature which crosses the barrier between the surrounding fields and us. I am sure that the word has spread because, in the quiet of night, I can hear almost every sound of every animal in every situation. Sometimes, the sound is of one creature killing another, such as the fox and the rabbit. But it is part of the system and I am glad that so much of it is played out in my garden and that even death is brought about by nature and not by man.

It is spring now. The sanctuary is filled with mother ducks, mother geese, mother this and mother that. Each one followed by their little feathered army of offspring. Since 'Him' and I parted we have exchanged birthday cards, Christmas cards and pretended 'Hail' and 'Hearty' phone calls. Each one keeping hold of something that won't go away.

When I was first asked to write this book, my thoughts were, 'Can I write a book? Am I capable of writing a book? Why should anybody think that I could write a book?' And then I remembered a very, very dear friend, who shall remain nameless – a brilliant writer who used to visit my flat and who treated me to conversations that I never tired of. One day, sitting beside me on the sofa as usual, each with our coffee, he suddenly requested to visit the bathroom. A few minutes later, he came to sit beside me again – he was naked. There was complete silence; we were both staring ahead. I sipped my coffee, so did he, and then, in an effort to end this strangest of all strange incidents and without looking at him, I whispered, 'I have a partner.' For a moment – nothing, and then he said, 'We have to try, don't we?' and he got up and went back to the bathroom.

When I picked up my pen to start this book with a large amount of self-doubt, I remembered his words, 'We have to try, don't we?'

Thoughts
Think of the plight of the fox in flight
The beast in the slaughterhouse
Hear their call as the hunted fall
And the cry of the scientists mouse

CARLA LANE

WRITING AWARDS AND HONOURS

Honours

OBE awarded in 1989. Returned in 2002.

Television Awards

The Pie Comedy Script Award 1981
The Pie Comedy Script Award 1971
Television Situation Comedy of the Year Award for *Bread* 1988
The Royal Television Society Hall of Fame for Outstanding Contribution
to British Television 1995
EMI (America) Award for *Butterflies*

Television Credits

1969–79, 96	*The Liver Birds* (with Myra Taylor)
1971-76	*Bless This House* (with Myra Taylor and others)
1974	*No Strings*
1975	*Going, Going, Gone . . . Free?*
1977	*Three Piece Suite*

1978-82, 2000	*Butterflies*
1981-83	*The Last Song*
1981-82	*Solo*
1984-85	*Leaving*
1985-87	*The Mistress*
1985	*I Woke Up One Morning*
1986-91	*Bread*
1993-94	*Luv*
1995	*Searching*

Animal Welfare Awards

Golden Bone Award 2000
Pride of Britain Award for Animal Welfare 2003

INDEX